AQA Religious Studies
St Mark's Gospel

Francis Loftus

Series editor
Cynthia Bartlett

OXFORD
UNIVERSITY PRESS

OXFORD
UNIVERSITY PRESS

Great Clarendon Street, Oxford, OX2 6DP, United Kingdom

Oxford University Press is a department of the University of Oxford. It furthers the University's objective of excellence in research, scholarship, and education by publishing worldwide. Oxford is a registered trade mark of Oxford University Press in the UK and in certain other countries

British Library Cataloguing in Publication Data
Data available

978-0-19-837039-0

Kerboodle book: 978-019-841270-0

10 9 8 7 6 5 4 3

Paper used in the production of this book is a natural, recyclable product made from wood grown in sustainable forests. The manufacturing process conforms to the environmental regulations of the country of origin.

Printed and bound by CPI Group (UK) Ltd, Croydon, CR0 4YY

Links to third party websites are provided by Oxford in good faith and for information only. Oxford disclaims any responsibility for the materials contained in any third party website referenced in this work.

Approval message from AQA

This textbook has been approved by AQA for use with our qualification. This means that we have checked that it broadly covers the specification and we are satisfied with the overall quality. Full details of our approval process can be found on our website.

We approve textbooks because we know how important it is for teachers and students to have the right resources to support their teaching and learning. However, the publisher is ultimately responsible for the editorial control and quality of this book.

Please note that when teaching the AQA GCSE Religious Studies course, you must refer to AQA's specification as your definitive source of information. While this book has been written to match the specification, it cannot provide complete coverage of every aspect of the course.

A wide range of other useful resources can be found on the relevant subject pages of our website: www.aqa.org.uk.

Please note that the Practice Questions in this book allow students a genuine attempt at practising exam skills, but they are not intended to replicate examination papers.

Contents

PART TWO: ST MARKS' GOSPEL AS A SOURCE OF RELIGIOUS, MORAL AND SPIRITUAL TRUTHS

Chapter 4: The Kingdom of God

Chapter 5: Jesus' relationships with those disregarded by society

Chapter 6: Faith and discipleship

Acknowledgements

The publisher would like to thank the following for permissions to use their photographs:

COVER: Baptism of Jesus, Stained-glass window (photo) / Godong/ UIG / Bridgeman Images; **p11**: Yan Vugenfirer/Shutterstock; **p12**: Dan Porges/Getty Images; **p13**: ZU_09/Getty Images; **p14**: World History Archive/Alamy Stock Photo; **p15**: Network Photographer/Alamy Stock Photo; **p16**: Medici/Mary Evans Picture Library; **p17**: Guild of Health and St. Raphael; **p18**: Maor Winetrob/Shutterstock; **p19**: Sopotnicki/ Shutterstock; **p20**: Godong/UIG/REX Shutterstock; **p21**: Open Doors; **p22**: Zvonimir Atletic/Shutterstock; **p23**: Mark Bassett/Alamy Stock Photo; **p24**: Yuriy Chertok/Shutterstock; **p25**: Irina Mos/Shutterstock; **p26**: Blueenayim/Dreamstime; **p27**: Zvonimir Atletic/Shutterstock; **p28**: Zoonar GmbH/Alamy Stock Photo; **p29**: www.BibleLandPictures. com/Alamy Stock Photo; **p31**: Epa european pressphoto agency b.v./ Alamy Stock Photo; **p32**: Chronicle/Alamy Stock Photo; **p33**: Dennis Cox/Alamy Stock Photo; **p34**: Sarah2/Shutterstock; **p35**: Friedrich Stark/ Alamy Stock Photo; **p37**: Renata Sedmakova/Shutterstock; **p38**: Francis Loftus; **p39**: JLBvdWOLF/Alamy Stock Photo; **p40**: S1001/Shutterstock; **p41**: SuperStock/Getty Images; **p42**: © Heritage Image Partnership Ltd / Alamy Stock Photo; **p43**: INTERFOTO / Alamy Stock Photo; **p45**: Renata Sedmakova/Shutterstock; **p46**: Francis Loftus; **p53**: Catalin Petolea/Shutterstock; **p54**: Perutskyi Petro/Shutterstock; **p54**: Jeka84/ Shutterstock **p55**: www.yqlcw.com; **p56**: Olgaman/Shutterstock; **p56**: Rhapsode/arabianEye/Getty Images; **p58**: Suffer the Little Children to Come Unto Me, 1538 (oil on panel), Cranach, Lucas, the Elder (1472-1553) / Hamburger Kunsthalle, Hamburg, Germany / Bridgeman Images; **p59**: David Bratley/Alamy Stock Photo; **p60**: Thinkstock; **p61**: Diego Cervo/Shutterstock; **p62**: Oculo/Shutterstock; **p63**: Patrick Poendl/ Shutterstock; **p64**: Sylvain Leser/Le Pictorium/Alamy; **p65**: Courtesy Hopegivers International; **p66**: The Calling of St. Matthew, illustration for 'The Life of Christ', c.1886-94 (w/c & gouache on paperboard), Tissot, James Jacques Joseph (1836-1902) / Brooklyn Museum of Art, New York, USA / Bridgeman Images; **p67**: Ethan Miller/Getty Images; **p68**: Cecilia Beltran/Alamy; **p70**: BlueSkyImage/Shutterstock; **p71**: Hans Wild/The LIFE Picture Collection/Getty Images; **p72**: Sean Pavone/Shutterstock; **p73**: PA Archive/Press Association Images; **p74**: Peter Horree/Alamy; **p75**: Hiroko Tanaka/Alamy; **p76**: Thomas Nebbia/National Geographic Creative/Alamy; **p77**: PA Archive/Press Association Images; **p78**: The Healing of the Woman with an Issue of Blood, William Blake (1757-1827)/Victoria & Albert Museum, London/Bridgeman Images; **p79**: Evgeny Shmulev/Shutterstock; **p81**: Michael Debets/Alamy; **p81**: Getty Images Sport; **p83**: ullstein bild/Getty Images; **p84**: Zvonimir Atletic/ Shutterstock; **p85**: S.Borisov/Shutterstock; **p86**: jorisvo/Shutterstock; **p87**: Pontino/Alamy;

We are grateful to the authors and publishers for use of extracts from their titles and in particular for the following:

The Scripture quotations contained herein are from the **New Revised Standard Version Bible**, copyright © 1989, Division of Christian Education of the National Council of Churches of Christ in the U.S.A. Used by permission. All rights reserved. The New Revised Standard Version Catholic Edition of the Bible, Harper Catholic Bibles – a division of Harper Collins.; Excerpts from **Catechism of the Catholic Church**, http://www.vatican.va/archive/ccc_css/archive/catechism/ ccc_toc.htm (Strathfield, NSW: St Pauls, 2000). © Libreria Editrice Vaticana. Copyright holder not established at time of going to print.; **D. Green:** *quote*, (Green, 2016). Reproduced with permission from David Green, Hobby Lobby Stores Founder and CEO.; **Bishop H. Montefiore:** *On Being a Jewish Christian*, (Hodder and Stoughton, 1998). Copyright © 1998 Hugh Montefiore. Reproduced with permission from Hodder and Stoughton Ltd.; **Bishop H. Montefiore:** *On Being a Jewish Christian*, (Hodder and Stoughton, 1998). Copyright © 1998 Hugh Montefiore. Reproduced with permission from Hodder and Stoughton Ltd.; **Archbishop W. Temple:** *quote*, 1942, (Lambeth Palace, 1942). Reproduced with permission from Lambeth Palace.; **Archbishop J. Welby:** *Christmas Day Sermon*, 25th December 2015, (Lambeth Palace, 2016). Reproduced with permission from Lambeth Palace.

We have made every effort to trace and contact all copyright holders before publication, but if notified of any errors or omissions, the publisher will be happy to rectify these at the earliest opportunity.

The author would like to thank his wife, Margaret Loftus, who helped with the first draft of this book.

The publishers would like to thank the following people for their valuable advice: Dr Debbie Herring, Revd Dr Mark Griffiths, and Philip Robinson, RE Adviser to the Catholic Education Service.

Introduction

This book can be used by GCSE students studying both Christianity for AQA Religious Studies Specification A and Catholic Christianity for specification B.

Chapter 1 covers St Mark's Gospel: the life of Jesus (3.2.2.1 Theme G in specification A and 3.2.2.4 Theme D in specification B), looking at the ministry of Jesus and his final days in Jerusalem.

Chapter 2 covers St Mark's Gospel as a source of religious, moral and spiritual truths (3.2.2.2 Theme H in specification A and 3.2.2.5 Theme E in specification B) and looks at ideas about the Kingdom of God, Jesus' relationships with those disregarded by society, faith and discipleship.

For a full course qualification in Specification A, the study of Mark's Gospel is combined with the study of Christianity, a second world religion, and two philosophical and ethical themes (Themes A–F). There are two examination papers, one on the religions, and the other on the themes and St Mark's Gospel.

Assessment guidance

Each chapter has an assessment guidance section that helps you to test your knowledge and understanding. There are multiple choice questions worth 1 mark, short-answer questions worth 2 marks, and longer questions worth 4 and 5 marks that test your ability to retell and explain facts. There are longer evaluation questions worth 12 marks that test your ability to analyse and evaluate different viewpoints.

Examination questions will test two assessment objectives, each representing 50 per cent of the total marks:

AO1: Demonstrate knowledge and understanding of religion and beliefs including:

- beliefs, practices and sources of authority
- influence on individuals, communities and societies
- similarities and differences within and/or between religions and beliefs.

AO2: Analyse and evaluate aspects of religion and belief, including their significance and influence.

For AO1 questions, the grid below gives guidance on how marks will be allocated:

Marks	Question type	Criteria
1 mark	Multiple choice	The correct answer chosen from 4 options
2 marks	Short answer (asking for two facts)	One mark for each of two correct points
4 marks	Asking for two Christian beliefs on an issue relating to St Mark's Gospel	For each of the two beliefs • one mark for a simple explanation of a relevant and accurate belief; • two marks for a detailed explanation of a relevant and accurate belief
5 marks	Asking for two ways in which an issue relating to St Mark's Gospel is important for Christians today PLUS specific reference to St Mark's Gospel	For each of the two ways: • one mark for a simple explanation of a relevant and way; • two marks for a detailed explanation of a relevant and accurate way; PLUS one mark for a relevant, accurate reference to St Mark's Gospel

The grid below gives you some guidance on the sort of quality expected at different levels for the 12-mark evaluation question (testing AO2).

Levels	Criteria	Marks
4	A well-argued response, reasoned consideration of different points of view	10–12
	Logical chains of reasoning leading to judgement(s) supported by knowledge and understanding of relevant evidence and information	
3	Reasoned consideration of different points of view	7–9
	Logical chains of reasoning that draw on knowledge and understanding of relevant evidence and information	
2	Reasoned consideration of a point of view	4–6
	A logical chain of reasoning drawing on knowledge and understanding of relevant evidence and information	
	OR	
	Recognition of different points of view, each supported by relevant reasons / evidence	
1	Point of view with reason(s) stated in support	1–3
0	Nothing worthy of credit	0

For the latest mark schemes, please also refer to the AQA website.

Examination grades will be awarded on a scale of 9–1 rather than A* to G. Grade 9 will be the equivalent of a new grade for high performing students above the current A*. Grade 4 will be the same as a grade C pass. The aim of the new grading system is to show greater differentiation between higher and lower achieving students.

Kerboodle Book

An online version of this book is available for student access, with an added bank of tools for you to personalise the book.

kerboodle

Part 1: The life of Jesus

1 The early ministry of Jesus

1.1 Background to Mark's Gospel

■ The history of Mark's Gospel

Mark's Gospel is one of four **gospels** in the New Testament (the others are Matthew, Luke and John). They were written in Greek, the language of the Roman Empire. A gospel is a very distinctive piece of writing. It is part biography, telling the story of the life of Jesus, and partly a way of teaching the Christian beliefs about Jesus – that he was the Messiah (Christ), the Son of God, who died on a cross and rose from the dead. The important questions are whether the gospels have authority and what is their importance both for the early Christians and for Christians today.

■ Mark's Gospel as the Word of God

The word 'gospel' means 'good news'. Christians believe that the authors of the gospels were inspired by God to write about the life of Jesus; the 'good news' which early Christian preachers were bringing to many of those who were hearing it. Some believe that the Gospel is the Word of God in the sense that it was dictated by the **Holy Spirit**. Others believe that, while the writers were inspired, their writing reflected their own personal interpretation of the life and teaching of Jesus.

■ The authority of the Gospel

The authority of the Gospel comes from the fact that it deals with the life of Jesus and Christians believe that it is an account of the life of the Son of God, God revealing himself in a unique way to humans. It is likely that after Jesus' death, as the early Christians began to preach about Jesus, that stories about Jesus and his teachings were passed around by word of mouth. It is possible that the gospel writers took information from this oral tradition.

Mark's Gospel is thought to be the earliest of the gospels, written between 65 and 70 CE, and is the gospel that is nearest to the events it describes. Many Christians believe that the gospels contain the actual words of Jesus – a few of which are included in Mark's Gospel in Aramaic, the language Jesus would have spoken. The authority also stems from the belief that Mark got his information from eyewitnesses, in particular the first **disciples** of Jesus. After the resurrection they became known as '**apostles**'.

Many scholars accept that while the Gospel is inspired and carries much authority, it was written by a human being about 35 years after the events. So it is possible that people's memories might not be entirely accurate and that different people remember different things.

In studying a gospel, it is important to understand the background of the time in which it was written, the people it was written for and the reasons why it was written. So it needs careful study and interpretation.

Within the Gospel, Jesus' divine authority is emphasised through accounts of his teachings and healings. Examples include the incident in the synagogue, where Jesus taught from the reading in Isaiah (Mark 1:21–25) and claimed that he was fulfilling the prophecy, and the calming of the storm (Mark 4:35–41) when the disciples believed his power came from God. At regular intervals in Mark's Gospel the people around Jesus question his authority, and his replies give Christians answers which help them to accept the authority of the Gospel.

■ Authorship and place of writing

It is thought that the Gospel was written by John Mark. He is sometimes thought to be the young man who saw Jesus arrested in the Garden of Gethsemane (Mark 14:51–52). It has been suggested that Jesus held the Last Supper at Mark's mother's house. However this is one of many theories about the authorship of the Gospel.

Most scholars think that Mark's Gospel was written in Rome to support persecuted Christians there. It is also believed that he wrote from the memories of the disciple, Peter. There are several reasons for this. For example, there is evidence that Peter was in Rome and possibly under arrest at this time. Some incidents are recorded at which only Peter was present, e.g. the denials (Mark 14:66–72), and others for which Peter was one of few disciples present, e.g. the transfiguration (Mark 9:2–8). Also, Peter is mentioned more times than any other disciple in Mark's Gospel. Some evidence for this theory comes from Papias, whose writings were quoted by Eusebius, an early Church historian:

> **❝** The Elder [Papias] also said this, 'Mark, became Peter's interpreter, and wrote accurately what he remembered ... For Mark had not heard the Lord, nor had he followed him, but later on, as I said, followed Peter ...' **❞**
>
> *Eusebius Ecclesiastical History*, 3.39.15

There are also signs that the Gospel was influenced or written by someone who knew Greek and had a Jewish background (this could have been Mark himself or eyewitnesses he consulted). In the Gospel there are Aramaic words which needed to be translated. There are also references to Jewish traditions which had to be explained.

■ Palestine in the time of Jesus

Mark's Gospel gives us no information about the birth of Jesus. It is very clear, though, that he was brought up in Nazareth in Galilee (Mark 1:9,24). It is likely that he was born some time around 4 BCE, and his ministry was some time between 27 CE and 33 CE. At the time the whole of Palestine was part of the Roman Empire. The ruler of Galilee during Jesus' life was King Herod, who was appointed by the Romans.

Research activities

1 Make a table of all the incidents that involve Peter in Mark's Gospel and note what his role was.

2 It is thought that Mark's Gospel was written to support early Christians being persecuted by the Romans. Find out about the persecution of Christians during Nero's reign in 64–68 CE.

▲ *This map shows what Palestine looked like during the Roman rule*

★ Study tip

Reading the whole of Mark's Gospel on your own will help you to understand the passages studied in detail later.

Summary
You should now understand the background, importance and authority of Mark's Gospel.

Mark's Gospel begins with a description of Jesus as the 'Son of God'. Other titles for Jesus are used as the Gospel progresses. Each has its own importance and indicates a different feature of Jesus' ministry.

■ Son of God

Son of God is the most important title that Mark uses for Jesus. It begins the Gospel and, towards the end, a centurion declares at the crucifixion, 'Surely this man was the Son of God' (15:39). The title is also used in the baptism (1:11) and the transfiguration (9:7), in which a voice from heaven describes Jesus as 'my son'. Finally, in the chapter on the trial before the Sanhedrin, Jesus is asked directly if he is the 'son of the blessed one' (the 'blessed one' means God) and he replies, 'I am' (14:61–62) Jesus is depicted in Mark's Gospel as having authority. This stems from Mark's certainty that in everything Jesus does, he is demonstrating God's power as his Son. However, Jesus did not refer to himself as the Son of God.

Jews who were true to their faith were called sons of God, and in the Old Testament the king was regarded as a son of God. Nevertheless, for Mark, Jesus had a unique relationship with God and the title suggests he was far more than just a good Jew.

■ Christ (Messiah)

Messiah is the Hebrew term for the 'anointed one'. The kings of Israel in the Old Testament were anointed with oil as part of their ceremony of kingship. Others too, such as high priests or occasionally prophets, were anointed, and it meant that they were set apart from other people or made holy. It was believed that the Messiah would be from that tradition. 'Christ' is the Greek translation of the word Messiah ('christos').

Jews believed that the Messiah would be descended from King David. David is regarded as the most important king in Jewish tradition. In his lifetime he established Jerusalem as the capital of the nation and his son, Solomon, built the first Temple.

Once Jews no longer had kings in the second century BCE, some people began to think of the Messiah, who would be a supernatural figure sent by God to bring in an age of justice and peace. Some Jews in the first century believed that the Messiah would be a warrior. They hoped that the Messiah would come and overthrow the Romans. They were so convinced of the role of the Messiah in removing the Romans that various rebel groups rebelled, until war broke out in Israel between the Jews and the Romans in 66 CE.

The title 'Messiah' was dangerous for Jesus. Although he never denied the validity of this title, he did not use it and did not want others to use it. He might have been arrested for using this term, so it could have ended his ministry too early. To claim to be the Messiah would have made him

Objective

● Understand the titles given to Jesus in Mark's Gospel and their importance.

Key terms

● **Son of God:** a title used for Jesus, the second person of the Trinity; denotes the special relationship between Jesus and God the Father

● **Christ (Messiah):** 'the anointed one'; a leader of the Jews who is expected to live on earth at some time in the future

● **blasphemy:** a religious offence which includes claiming to be God

● **Messianic Secret:** a characteristic of Mark's Gospel where Jesus does not wish to be recognised as the Messiah

● **Son of Man:** a title that could refer to either just a human being, or a human who is given power by God

Activities

1 List all the extracts from Mark's Gospel where the phrase 'Son of Man' is used. What do they tell you about Jesus' authority and his role?

2 From your list, explain how Jesus is seen as a saviour.

seem a threat to the Romans and would have led to misinterpretation of his work. It would have been regarded as **blasphemy** to claim to be related to God. Blasphemy was punishable by death (even though the Jews technically could not use the death penalty).

This led to a theory about 'the **Messianic Secret**' – that Jesus did not want people to know that he was the Messiah. He sometimes told people not to talk about healings, and in the villages of Caesarea Philippi he told the disciples to say nothing after Peter had declared that Jesus was the Christ.

■ Son of David

All Jewish men are sons of David – named after King David. In this sense the phrase has a general meaning. However, to be called the Son of David had messianic overtones. In Mark 10:46–52, Jesus is called Son of David by the blind man Bartimaeus.

■ Son of Man

The title '**Son of Man**' is found in the Old Testament. The first meaning of 'son of man' is just 'a man', a human being. In the Old Testament the book of Ezekiel uses this term most frequently – God calls the prophet Ezekiel 'son of man' many times. In the Book of Daniel, however, the Son of Man comes with the 'clouds of heaven'. (Daniel 7: 13)

The title is also found in other Jewish literature, where the meaning is much more mysterious. While it is not a messianic title, it is associated with a heavenly being of great power who would appear when the world was going to be judged by God.

This was the title Jesus used for himself most often – in Mark's Gospel it is used 14 times. It was a safe title in many ways. Those who heard him would have thought he was just talking about himself or another person, whereas Jesus' followers would have linked it with the Old Testament meaning of one coming with power at the end of time.

In Mark's Gospel, Jesus sometimes uses the phrase 'Son of Man' to show that he came to serve (Mark 10:45).

■ The use by Christians of titles for Jesus

Most Christians today believe that Jesus was both a real human being, sent by God, and at the same time, the Son of God, God Himself, having powers that only God has. The title 'Son of Man', though it is not commonly used today, helps Christians to understand that Jesus was a man, fully human. It helps them to identify with his humanity. Christians believe that Jesus was a descendant of David who demonstrated God's power – particularly by rising from the dead. He fulfilled the Old Testament predictions that he would teach, serve and suffer. Christians often use the Greek word for Messiah, 'Christ', to describe Jesus. This is the title that is used throughout the Epistles and the Acts of the Apostles in the New Testament. Whichever title modern Christians use, all the titles used by Mark were meant to emphasise Jesus' authority and his role.

▲ *The Tower of David in Jerusalem is named after King David*

Links

For Daniel 7:13 see page 41. See pages 32–33 for the healing of Bartimaeus.

Research activity

Collect different images of Jesus from around the world. What do they tell you about people's beliefs in who Jesus was?

> **❝** So the Son of Man is lord even of the sabbath. **❞**
> *Mark* 2:28 [NRSV]

⭐ Study tip

It is important that you learn the different titles that Jesus is given in Mark's Gospel and their importance in a Christian understanding of Jesus.

Summary

You should now know about the titles of Jesus in Mark's Gospel and their importance in understanding who Jesus was.

John's preparation for Jesus' ministry – Mark 1:1–8

> **"** The beginning of the good news of Jesus Christ, the Son of God.
>
> As it is written in the prophet Isaiah,
>
> 'See, I am sending my messenger ahead of you,
>
> who will prepare your way;
>
> the voice of one crying out in the wilderness:
>
> "Prepare the way of the Lord,
>
> make his paths straight"',
>
> John the baptiser appeared in the wilderness, proclaiming a **baptism** of **repentance** for the forgiveness of sins. And people from the whole Judean countryside and all the people of Jerusalem were going out to him, and were baptised by him in the river Jordan, confessing their sins. Now John was clothed with camel's hair, with a leather belt around his waist, and he ate locusts and wild honey. He proclaimed, 'The one who is more powerful than I is coming after me; I am not worthy to stoop down and untie the thong of his sandals. I have baptised you with water; but he will baptise you with the Holy Spirit.' **"**
>
> *Mark* 1:1–8 [NRSV]

Objectives

- Study the work of John the Baptist as the forerunner of Jesus.
- Understand the importance of baptism in the first century CE.

Key terms

- **baptism:** a cleansing to show repentance; an initiation ceremony using water; in the time of Jesus, this meant being completely submerged in water for a brief time.
- **repentance:** saying sorry, and a way of believers acknowledging to God that things have gone wrong

■ The introduction

Mark wastes no time in telling his readers what his gospel is about: 'The beginning of the good news of Jesus Christ, the Son of God' (Mark 1:1). The name 'Jesus' in Hebrew would be 'Yehoshua' (in English, 'Joshua') and means 'God is salvation'. Mark is making it clear that Jesus has come from God to save people. This is intended to give hope to believers.

The title 'Christ' is not often used in Mark's Gospel, but Mark wanted to make this belief clear at the beginning. The promise that the Messiah, a descendant of King David, would come to save the people, is based on Old Testament tradition. Joseph was a descendant of David (Matthew 1:20), and so Jesus was of David's family.

■ John the Baptist

John the Baptist is an important person in Christian belief. He was a strange-looking figure, with his dress of camel's hair and a leather belt. It is thought that he may at some point have been a member of the Qumran Community (referred to as The Essenes). This was a Jewish monastery in the Judean Desert near the Dead Sea.

▲ *John baptised in the River Jordan*

John's role, according to Mark's Gospel, is to prepare the way for Jesus' coming. His message that he was a forerunner to Jesus was clear. Mark quotes from the prophet Isaiah (40:3) to make the link to the Old Testament. He is saying that Jesus is the one God promised to send, and John is the messenger who will announce his coming.

Judaism teaches that the forerunner to the Messiah will be the prophet Elijah. Mark suggests that John the Baptist is like Elijah, preparing the way for the coming of the Messiah.

■ Baptism

The use of water as a sign of repentance (to turn away from sins and commit to a life of God) and making a new beginning was well established. In Qumran, near the Dead Sea, archaeologists have found the remains of a number of baptisteries – pools constructed for baptism. John performed baptisms in River Jordan, which runs through the Judean Desert into the Dead Sea. Some scholars believe that he may have been influenced by the beliefs and practices of the community living in Qumran.

It is assumed that John only baptised adults. However, we know that the early disciples baptised whole families which may have included children and babies. Today some Christian churches baptise adults, as John did, and other churches baptise babies as well. The symbolism is similar – it is the sign of a new beginning. For Christians it is a symbol of entry into life in a Christian community.

■ John's preparation for Jesus

John taught the people about the need to ask forgiveness for sins and, once baptised, begin a new life. He also announced the coming of one who was much greater than him. He was the forerunner to Jesus, preparing people to hear Jesus' message. John taught that Jesus would be the one to give all Christian believers the gift of the Holy Spirit.

The Holy Spirit is the third person of the Trinity. Christians believe that God is the Father, the Son and the Holy Spirit. The Holy Spirit appears in the creation narrative of Genesis 1 and is said to be the power of creation. Throughout the Bible it is said that the spirit of God is given to people. This will give them the power to withstand and overcome persecution but also a certainty that God is with them at all times.

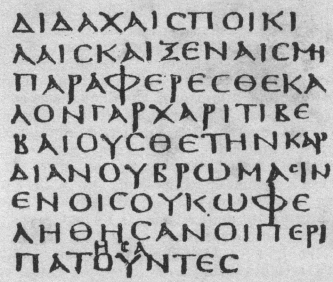

▲ *The Codex Sinaiticus, a very early version of the Bible, contains the earliest complete Gospel of Mark.*

Links

See pages 14–15 and 58–59 for more on baptism.

Activities

1 What does Mark 1:1 teach about Jesus?

2 'John the Baptist's work was essential to prepare the way for Jesus' ministry.' Do you agree? Give reasons for your answer.

3 What is the importance of baptism for Christians today?

⭐ Study tip

It is important to understand that John the Baptist was the forerunner to Jesus and some thought that he was like Elijah, the prophet.

Summary

You should now have an understanding of the beginning of Mark's Gospel and the work of John the Baptist.

Research activity 🔍

Find out about the Qumran Community and their buildings. What did they believe about the Messiah? How might this have influenced John the Baptist?

Jesus' baptism and temptation – Mark 1:9–13

> **❝** In those days Jesus came from Nazareth of Galilee and was baptised by John in the Jordan. And just as he was coming up out of the water, he saw the heavens torn apart and the Spirit descending like a dove on him. And a voice came from heaven, 'You are my Son, the Beloved; with you I am well pleased.' And the Spirit immediately drove him out into the wilderness. He was in the wilderness for forty days, tempted by **Satan**; and he was with the wild beasts; and the angels waited on him. **❞**
>
> *Mark* 1:9–13 [NRSV]

Objective

- Consider the baptism and temptation of Jesus and understand their significance for Jesus and for Christians today.

Key term

- **Satan:** name for the Devil – the power and source of evil

Activity

Which of the symbols in the baptism of Jesus do you think are the most important? Explain your answer.

Mark mentions that Jesus came to John from Nazareth, the town where Jesus had grown up. According to Mark's Gospel, the baptism of Jesus marks the beginning of Jesus' public ministry, which many scholars believe took place between 27 and 30 CE.

■ The symbolism of the baptism of Jesus

Water

Jesus would have been well aware of the importance of water in his tradition. According to Genesis 1, in the beginning, before the earth was given any form, the Spirit of God hovered over the waters. Moses led the Israelites through the parted waters of the Red Sea as they escaped from Egypt. John was offering a baptism of repentance for the forgiveness of sins, and so water is a sign of new life and cleansing.

'Heavens torn apart'

This is a sign of God's presence. The prophet Isaiah spoke of the heavens being opened to allow for the coming of the Messiah. 'Torn apart' is a very strong phrase showing that this was an important event.

The dove

The text says that the Holy Spirit descended 'like a dove' (or in some versions 'in the form of a dove'). Most commentators believe that what Jesus saw was a dove. In an old Jewish commentary on the creation story in Genesis 1:2, the Spirit of God was likened to a dove. Noah released a dove at the end of the flood and it returned with an olive branch in its mouth. Noah then knew that the flood waters had gone. Doves were a sign of God's presence, and the peace which will be in God's Kingdom.

In Mark's account of the baptism of Jesus, the dove indicates the presence of God in the form of the Holy Spirit. It is as if the Holy Spirit is being given to Jesus to strengthen him for his temptations and then for his ministry.

▲ *A painting from the 14th century of John baptising Jesus. Jesus was baptised by John in the River Jordan; John was baptising in the River Jordan by total immersion, meaning a person's whole body was covered by the water*

The voice

While the text does not explicitly say that it is God speaking, the reader can safely assume this. In Jewish tradition the *bat qol* (voice of God from heaven) was used as proof of God's presence and affirmation. This is the first occasion in Mark when there is a voice from heaven, with God telling Jesus that he is his son and that he is 'well pleased' with him. It is not clear whether anyone else heard the voice. That the Messiah was regarded as God's son is foreshadowed in Psalm 2:7.

The temptations

Mark gives us no details at all about the temptations of Jesus. Yet the few words that are used indicate that Jesus really suffered. Mark says that the Spirit 'drove him out into the wilderness'. The reference to the 'wild beasts', which were sometimes thought to be demons opposing the will of God, again shows that this was a serious testing time for Jesus. Angels, on the other hand, were messengers of God, providing Jesus with support. Details of the temptations can be found in the Gospels of Luke and Matthew. For Mark, who is clearly keen to get on with the story of Jesus' actions, this short reference is enough.

> ❝ I will tell of the decree of the Lord: He said to me, 'You are my son; today I have begotten you.' ❞
>
> *Psalm 2:7* [NRSV]

Links

See pages 26–27 for another example where we hear the voice of God.

⭐ Study tip

Make sure you do not confuse Mark's account, particularly of the temptations, with Matthew or Luke's accounts of the temptations.

■ Baptism and temptation for twenty-first-century Christians

Many churches still use baptism as the beginning of a person's Christian commitment. Some people are baptised as babies and others as adults, as a way of saying that the person belongs to God. In the case of babies, godparents and parents make promises to bring the child up as a Christian. In the case of adults, they make these promises for themselves. Water is used in baptism today, and is a direct link with the baptism John was offering, and with Jesus' experiences. There are times when some Christians today believe that they have heard the voice of God and that this experience has changed their lives.

▲ *The baptism ceremony today connects Christians with Jesus' baptism. The Baptist Church baptises only adults by total immersion, covering the whole body with water*

Christians remember the temptations during the period of Lent in the Church's year – the 40 days before Easter. In the Gospels of Matthew and Luke reference is made to Jesus fasting (going without food) for 40 days, and in many traditions Christians give something up during Lent or do something extra, for example raising money for charity. It is a time of prayer and spiritual reflection, and a time for self-discipline – which is what Jesus would have experienced when in the wilderness.

Summary

You should now know about the baptism and temptations of Jesus as recorded in Mark and understand their significance for Jesus and for Christian practice today.

> When he returned to Capernaum after some days, it was reported that he was at home. So many gathered around that there was no longer room for them, not even in front of the door; and he was speaking the word to them. Then some people came, bringing to him a paralysed man, carried by four of them. And when they could not bring him to Jesus because of the crowd, they removed the roof above him; and after having dug through it, they let down the mat on which the paralytic lay. When Jesus saw their faith, he said to the paralytic, 'Son, your sins are forgiven.'
>
> Now some of the scribes were sitting there, questioning in their hearts, 'Why does this fellow speak in this way? It is blasphemy! Who can forgive sins but God alone?' At once Jesus perceived in his spirit that they were discussing these questions among themselves; and he said to them, 'Why do you raise such questions in your hearts? Which is easier, to say to the paralytic, "Your sins are forgiven", or to say, "Stand up and take your mat and walk"? But so that you may know that the Son of Man has authority on earth to forgive sins'— he said to the paralytic—'I say to you, stand up, take your mat and go to your home.' And he stood up, and immediately took the mat and went out before all of them; so that they were all amazed and glorified God, saying, 'We have never seen anything like this!'
>
> *Mark* 2:1–12 [NRSV]

Objectives

- Know the account of the healing of the paralysed man.
- Understand what the story teaches about the authority of Jesus.

Key term

- **miracle:** a seemingly impossible event, usually good, that cannot be explained by natural or scientific laws, and is thought to be the action of God

Activities

1 Read the extract from Mark 2:1–12. Explain the reaction of the different groups to this miracle.

2 Do people still believe that sin leads to suffering? Ask people you know what their view is.

▲ *The men broke open the flat roof to get the paralysed man to Jesus inside the house*

There are a number of things to note in the incident from Mark 2:1–12. The first is the place of faith. We cannot tell from the text whether the paralysed man had faith or not. It is possible that he had. It is likely that Jesus was developing as a teacher and healer, and the men who brought the paralysed man believed that Jesus could cure him. They had so much faith that they dismantled the roof to get to Jesus. In many of the healing miracles of Jesus, faith in him is demonstrated by those who wish to be cured or by those who wish to have loved ones cured.

At the time of Jesus, many Jews believed that sin led to suffering, and that suffering was therefore a punishment for sin. So if Jesus forgave the man's sins he would be cured of his illness.

■ Conflict

This miracle shows the authority of Jesus, but Jesus came into conflict with the teachers of the law at this point. They did not say anything, but Jesus knew that they were unhappy. They believed that only God could forgive sins. Who was Jesus to claim to be able to do this? They concluded that he was therefore making himself like God and committing blasphemy. However, Jesus told the man to get up and walk and the man did so.

 The logo of the Guild of Health and St Raphael shows the angel helping a Jew named Tobit to catch a fish with healing powers

■ Authority

Jesus acted with authority on this occasion. He demonstrated authority over the illness of the man by curing him. He also showed in his teaching that he had the authority and the power to forgive sins. Notice how in Mark's account he uses the title of himself 'Son of Man'. This has the effect of claiming to be sent by God without actually stating it.

However, the reaction of the crowd emphasises the authority of Jesus. They claim that they 'have never seen anything like this'. This is an interesting reaction, because at the time of Jesus there were other Galilean teachers who could perform miracles, such as Hanina ben Dosa. Yet the crowd here see something different in Jesus. This amazement is one of the things that Mark records time and again in his gospel. Throughout the Gospel, Jesus' authority is supported by his actions and teachings, and recognised by others.

Early Christians who read Mark's Gospel during times of persecution would have been comforted to know that Jesus had authority from God to forgive sins and to heal.

> **Research activity** 🔍
>
> There is a strong tradition of healing in the Christian Church. Find out about the work of the Guild of Health and St Raphael.

> **Links**
>
> See pages 10–11 for more on Jesus' use of the title 'Son of Man'.

> ⭐ **Study tip**
>
> Make sure that you can recall accurately the details of this event as Mark records it especially the words of Jesus.

> **Summary**
>
> You should now know an example from Mark's Gospel of a healing miracle which demonstrated Jesus' authority.

The healing of Jairus' daughter – Mark 5:21–24a, 35–43

> ❝ When Jesus had crossed again in the boat to the other side, a great crowd gathered round him; and he was beside the lake. Then one of the leaders of the synagogue named Jairus came and, when he saw him, fell at his feet, and begged him repeatedly, 'My little daughter is at the point of death. Come and lay your hands on her, so that she may be made well, and live.' So he went with him …
>
> While he was still speaking, some people came from the leader's house to say, 'Your daughter is dead. Why trouble the teacher any further?' But overhearing what they said, Jesus said to the leader of the synagogue, 'Do not fear, only believe.' He allowed no one to follow him except Peter, James, and John, the brother of James. When they came to the house of the leader of the synagogue, he saw a commotion, people weeping and wailing loudly. When he had entered, he said to them, 'Why do you make a commotion and weep? The child is not dead but sleeping.' And they laughed at him. Then he put them all outside, and took the child's father and mother and those who were with him, and went in where the child was. He took her by the hand and said to her, 'Talitha cum', which means, 'Little girl, get up!' And immediately the girl got up and began to walk about (she was twelve years of age). At this they were overcome with amazement. He strictly ordered them that no one should know this, and told them to give her something to eat. ❞
>
> *Mark 5:21–24a, 35–43* [NRSV]

Objectives

- Learn about the healing of Jairus' daughter.
- Understand the role of faith in the cure.

Key terms

- **the twelve:** the title given to Jesus' disciples as a group
- **synagogue:** a place of meeting for Jewish believers where the scrolls of the Law are kept

Links

See pages 68–69 for an example of Jesus healing without using touch.

It is interesting to note that, although Jesus often found himself in conflict with those in authority, on this occasion it was one of the **synagogue** leaders who came to Jesus seeking help. This is not so surprising since we know that Jesus spent time in the synagogue at Capernaum and would have been well known there (Mark 1:21).

■ Faith

Jairus demonstrated faith in Jesus. He found Jesus and showed how desperate he was for his daughter to be cured. Jesus did not hesitate, but went with him. Jairus believed that Jesus needed to touch the little girl to cure her. In another healing Jesus did not need to even see the sick child (e.g. the Syro-Phoenician woman's daughter).

▲ *The Sea of Galilee*

■ Peter, James and John

Jesus had 12 disciples in his inner group, whose names are listed in Mark 3:16–19. They were known collectively as **the twelve**. However, on a number of occasions he took with him only Peter, James and John, and here they were witnesses to the healing of Jairus' daughter.

Mark's account of this miracle describes how Jesus made what appears to be an amazing statement. He told the wailing people that the girl was asleep, not dead. At this point he had not even seen her. The Aramaic phrase 'Talitha cum' is translated as, 'Little girl, get up!' This is evidence that the Gospel was aimed at non-Jewish (Gentile) believers, not just Jews. The word 'talitha' in Aramaic means 'little lamb', a very gentle way to describe a little girl. This is perhaps an example of an eyewitness account, because someone remembered the detail that the parents were told to give her something to eat.

The effect of Jesus taking the girl's hand was immediate and she was at once fully cured. This is another good example of where the authority of Jesus shows God's power for Mark and Christian believers. There is some debate about whether the girl was actually dead or just in a coma. For believers this does not matter – the girl was clearly very ill and Jesus cured her as result of her father's faith and his use of God's power.

▲ *The remains of a fourth-century synagogue in Capernaum, built on the site of an earlier one; Jairus was a leader of the synagogue*

In this narrative Jesus told the family not to tell anyone what had happened. This is one of the occasions which led to a belief in the Messianic Secret – the theory that Jesus did not want people to claim openly that he was the Messiah. It would have been dangerous for Jesus to be called the Messiah because he could have been accused of blasphemy.

Links

See pages 10–11 for more on the Messianic Secret.

Research activity 🔍

Research two other occasions in which Peter, James and John were with Jesus (Mark 9:2 and 14:32). Suggest reasons why Jesus may have wanted just three of his disciples present on these occasions.

Activities

1 What does this miracle show about Jesus' authority?
2 Do you think the little girl was dead? Do you think it makes a difference to believe in Jesus as healer if she was not dead?

Study tip

Learn both parts of this story as one incident, even though the Gospel includes another healing in the middle of it.

Summary

You should now know an example of a healing miracle which demonstrates faith, is an example of Jesus raising someone from the dead, and which led to the belief in the Messianic Secret.

> **❝** He left that place and came to his home town, and his disciples followed him. On the **sabbath** he began to teach in the synagogue, and many who heard him were astounded. They said, 'Where did this man get all this? What is this wisdom that has been given to him? What deeds of power are being done by his hands! Is not this the carpenter, the son of Mary and brother of James and Joses and Judas and Simon, and are not his sisters here with us?' And they took offence at him. Then Jesus said to them, 'Prophets are not without honour, except in their home town, and among their own kin, and in their own house.' And he could do no deed of power there, except that he laid his hands on a few sick people and cured them. And he was amazed at their unbelief. **❞**
>
> *Mark 6:1–6* [NRSV]

Objective

- Study the incident of the rejection at Nazareth and understand some of the reactions of people to Jesus.

Key term

- **sabbath (shabbat):** the Jewish holy day of the week; a day of spiritual renewal beginning at sunset on Friday and continuing to nightfall on Saturday

The reaction of the crowd is interesting here. They knew Jesus as the son of Mary and Joseph. The gospels report that Jesus was from Nazareth, so this was his hometown. He is described as a carpenter, and his brothers and sisters are named. Because some people believe that Mary remained a virgin, it is suggested that these brothers and sisters were in fact Joseph's children from an earlier marriage.

The crowd took offence – the Greek word is 'scandalised'. The word means a 'stumbling block' and is used eight times in Mark to indicate that people found Jesus' teaching difficult to accept, or they felt that it was inappropriate for Jesus to be teaching the way he did. The question 'Where did this man get all this?' links to the question asked by the disciples in the calming of the storm – 'Who then is this?' (Mark 4:41). Questioning who Jesus was and his authority was common at the time.

The statement that Jesus makes that 'Prophets are not without honour, except in their home town…' has become a proverb. It means that sometimes the people who have known a person and their family for a long time are those who find it the most difficult to accept that they are special, or have particular talents or abilities. They are more likely to question and doubt. Jesus was amazed at their lack of faith. This happened at other times in Jesus' ministry. In the calming of the storm Jesus asks the disciples, 'Have you still no faith?' (Mark 4:40).

▲ *It was normal for the men to read from the scriptures and speak in the synagogue and therefore not surprising or unusual that Jesus did so*

Brother Andrew

Brother Andrew was a Dutch monk who believed that it was his calling to go into the Communist countries of Europe after the Second World War and take Bibles. The possession of a Bible was a criminal offence at that time in some countries. From 1955 he visited Communist countries regularly. He was arrested on occasions and suffered for his beliefs and actions.

▲ Brother Andrew was given the nickname God's Smuggler

■ Persecution and rejection

Jesus experienced persecution and rejection. The early Christians also experienced persccution under Nero, particularly in Rome. That Jesus had suffered similar rejection would have given comfort and strength to those who were suffering.

Today the persecution of Christians is very common. In parts of Africa and the Middle East it is dangerous to practise Christianity. Churches have been attacked and Christians killed and arrested. In December 2015 the Archbishop of Canterbury stated that in the Middle East 'Christians face elimination in the very region in which Christian faith began'. This comment reflects years of persecution.

Research activity 🔍

Use the Internet (websites such as www.statista.com) to find out what it tells you about Christian persecution worldwide.

Activities

1 Why it important to Christians to believe that Jesus had similar experiences to those of others?
2 Should Brother Andrew have done what he did, given that he was breaking the law?

Summary

You should now have an understanding about Jesus' rejection at Nazareth and be able to make connections between this experience and those of Christians today.

⭐ Study tip

Get used to making links between the different stories and events that you study; look for common themes. It is helpful to be able to recall different examples from the Gospel to illustrate your answers.

> **"** The apostles gathered around Jesus, and told him all that they had done and taught. He said to them, 'Come away to a deserted place all by yourselves and rest a while.' For many were coming and going, and they had no leisure even to eat. And they went away in the boat to a deserted place by themselves. Now many saw them going, and recognized them, and they hurried there on foot from all the towns, and arrived ahead of them. As he went ashore, he saw a great crowd; and he had compassion for them, because they were like sheep without a shepherd; and he began to teach them many things.
>
> When it grew late, his disciples came to him and said, 'This is a deserted place, and the hour is now very late; send them away so that they may go into the surrounding country and villages and buy something for themselves to eat.' But he answered them, 'You give them something to eat.' They said to him, 'Are we to go and buy two hundred denarii worth of bread, and give it to them to eat?' And he said to them, 'How many loaves have you? Go and see.' When they had found out, they said, 'Five, and two fish.' Then he ordered them to get all the people to sit down in groups on the green grass. So they sat down in groups of hundreds and of fifties. Taking the five loaves and the two fish, he looked up to heaven, and blessed and broke the loaves, and gave them to the disciples to set before the people; and he divided the two fish among them all. And all ate and were filled; and they took up twelve baskets full of broken pieces and of the fish. Those who had eaten the loaves numbered five thousand men. **"**
>
> *Mark 6:30–44* [NRSV]

Objective

- Consider the account of the feeding of the 5000 and understand its significance in demonstrating the authority of Jesus.

Key term

- **Holy Communion:** the giving of bread and wine as a memorial of Jesus in church services; also referred to as Eucharist (thanksgiving), Mass or The Lord's Supper

Research activity

Find out about the work of CAFOD or Christian Aid and their work in feeding the hungry.

Jesus performed many miracles. Some were healing miracles, and he also raised two people from the dead. This incident in Mark 6:30–44 is an example of a nature miracle, in which the understood rules of nature seem to have been broken.

■ The disciples

In this passage, Mark describes how the disciples expressed concern about a practical matter. The people had clearly been with Jesus a long time and needed to eat something. Jesus immediately challenged the disciples to feed them themselves. The scale of this task is demonstrated by the disciples' protest that it would take half a year's wages (200 denarii) to feed such a crowd.

▲ *A mosaic in a church at Tabgha on the shore of Lake Galilee, created by Christians in the fifth century* CE

The disciples were then given tasks by Jesus: to find out what food they had – five loaves and two fish only – and to tell the crowds to sit in groups. People who saw the crowd sitting in large groups like this (of 50 or 100 people each) may have thought that they were like the army units mentioned in the Old Testament. Perhaps they thought that this showed the willingness of the people to support Jesus even, if necessary, against the Romans.

The disciples gave out the food and collected the scraps afterwards. In this they are like the deacons in the early Church. Early Christian readers of the Gospel would have been familiar with the deacons who worked in churches and helped with the meals. In Acts 6:2–6 seven deacons were appointed to meet the practical needs of members of the early Church so that the apostles could focus on preaching.

■ Understanding the symbolism of the meal

One interpretation of this meal event is that it shows that Jesus was like Moses. An Old Testament tradition said that God would raise up a prophet like Moses (Deuteronomy 18:15). Moses had prayed to God when the Israelites were in the Sinai Desert during their 40 years after leaving Egypt. God had then provided manna, a bread-like substance, and the people were fed. This feeding of 5000 people by Jesus in a deserted place is very similar.

 The church at Tabgha is believed to be on the site where the feeding of the 5000 took place

In the Old Testament it is promised that the Messiah would ensure that all were fed. It describes an image of the Messianic Banquet that all would share. The feeding of the 5000 can be seen as a symbol of this Messianic Banquet and therefore shows Jesus as the Messiah. He demonstrated God's power by miraculously feeding 5000 people with a small amount of food and ensuring that their physical, as well as their spiritual, needs were met.

The narrative contains much symbolism. The five loaves may represent the first five books of the Old Testament, known as the Torah or Law. The two fish could represent the two tablets on which the Ten Commandments were written. The 12 baskets of crumbs are often said to represent the 12 tribes of Israel.

There is another aspect of the feeding of the 5000 that may have been understood by the early Church. The text tells us that Jesus took the loaves and fish and gave thanks to God for them. He then broke the bread and gave it to the disciples to distribute. These actions are exactly what he did at the Last Supper – Jesus took the bread and gave thanks, broke it and gave it to his disciples. As Christians read this account today, many are reminded of their practice of meeting to share bread and wine in the **Holy Communion** service.

Some people may interpret this event as demonstrating Jesus' power to feed people physically, and, at the same time, to feed them spiritually through his teaching.

Discussion activity

'It is more important for Christians to feed the hungry than to preach.' Evaluate this statement. Give reasons for your answer, showing that you have thought about more than one point of view.

Links

See pages 36–37 for more on the Last Supper.

★ Study tip

Learn the details of this account as accurately as you can; this will help you to interpret it well.

Summary

You should now have knowledge of the feeding of the 5000 and be aware of its importance in understanding who Jesus was.

2.1 The conversation at Caesarea Philippi – Mark 8:27–33

> ❝ Jesus went on with his disciples to the villages of Caesarea Philippi; and on the way he asked his disciples, 'Who do people say that I am?' And they answered him, 'John the Baptist; and others, Elijah; and still others, one of the prophets.' He asked them, 'But who do you say that I am?' Peter answered him, 'You are the Messiah.' And he sternly ordered them not to tell anyone about him.
>
> Then he began to teach them that the Son of Man must undergo great suffering, and be rejected by the elders, the chief priests, and the scribes, and be killed, and after three days rise again. He said all this quite openly. And Peter took him aside and began to rebuke him. But turning and looking at his disciples, he rebuked Peter and said, 'Get behind me, Satan! For you are setting your mind not on divine things but on human things.' ❞
>
> *Mark 8:27–33* [NRSV]

Objective

● Learn about the conversation between Jesus and his disciples at Caesarea Philippi and understand its significance.

Key term

● **passion prediction**: a passage in Mark's Gospel where Jesus explains that he will suffer and die

Research activity

Compare Jesus' passion predictions with what happened to him after his arrest. You can find the passion predictions at Mark 8:31; 9:31; 10:33 and Jesus' arrest and afterwards in Mark 15:1–15.

■ The conversation at Caesarea Philippi

This conversation between Jesus and his disciples is one of the most important in the Gospel. They were in the area of Caesarea Philippi, which was a largely non-Jewish town in the north of Israel, near the border with Syria.

Jesus' question seems very simple: 'Who do people say that I am?' The apparent authority of Jesus' teaching, and the miracles he performed, had led people to speculate over who he was, but nobody had yet come to any conclusion.

Some people thought that Jesus might be John the Baptist. By this time, John had been beheaded by Herod, but some people may have thought that he had miraculously come back to life. Others thought Jesus was Elijah. Some Jews at the time believed that the Messiah might come to rescue Israel from the Roman occupation, and believed that Elijah would return as a forerunner to the Messiah. Some thought Jesus might be 'one of the prophets' because his teaching resembled the teaching of the Old Testament prophets, with his emphasis on justice and following God's commandments.

▲ *The ruins of a temple at Caesura Philippi, dedicated to the Greek god Pan*

■ 'You are the Messiah'

Jesus' next question, 'Who do you say that I am?' is very significant because it addresses his disciples' opinions directly. Peter seems to answer without hesitation, using the word 'Messiah'. This demonstrates Peter's central role in Mark's Gospel. It also creates an image of Peter as an impetuous disciple who was prone to making rash statements (e.g. Mark 14:31). However this does not take away the importance of this statement. According to Mark, Peter had recognised that Jesus was the promised Messiah (Christ) – something that, until this point in the Gospel, only God and demons had recognised.

Mark then explains that Jesus warned them to tell no one. This is another statement which has led to the theory of the Messianic Secret. To believe Jesus was the Messiah would have perhaps led to misunderstandings about his role, and might have attracted unwelcome attention, including even offers of support from those who wanted to fight against Roman rule.

■ Jesus' teaching about himself

Jesus then began to teach them about his destiny. Mark describes how Jesus used his favourite title for himself, Son of Man, and emphasised that his understanding of his messianic nature would involve suffering and self-sacrifice. This is sometimes called a 'passion prediction'.

According to Mark, when Peter disagreed, Jesus responded, 'Get behind me, Satan!' This is a harsh thing to say to a follower, but to Jesus Peter probably sounded like Satan in the desert, tempting and encouraging him to believe that there might be other ways to complete his work than suffering and death. Mark's Gospel does not provide the detail of the temptations (unlike in Luke's Gospel), but it is clear that Jesus must have been affected by the experience of the temptations. Mark records three occasions on which Jesus predicted his future suffering (Mark 8:31; 9:31; 10:33).

■ The importance of this event

Within the Gospel this event is a turning point, sometimes called a 'watershed moment'. A watershed moment is a point in someone's life when a change of direction happens. In this case; after this conversation:

- Jesus had less to do with the crowds and concentrated more on teaching the disciples.
- He set out for Jerusalem, the centre of religious and political power, and the place where he would die.
- The tone of the Gospel gets darker; Jesus was challenged more by those he met.

To the early Christians the event gave a clear message that Jesus was a suffering Messiah, and that followers of Jesus might be asked to suffer too. For believers today, this event gives great encouragement. It is clear from the words of Peter that Jesus was indeed the Messiah (Christ), sent by God to save the people, and this conversation established that belief early on.

▲ Peter was the first of the disciples to recognise Jesus as the Messiah

Links

See pages 38–39 for information about Jesus facing temptation in Gethsemane.

Activities

1 Why do you think Jesus asked, 'Who do people say that I am?'

2 How do you think Jesus would have felt when he heard Peter's answer to this question?

3 Explain why the conversation at Caesarea Philippi is important in Mark's Gospel.

★ Study tip

Try to learn and understand the meanings of the answers that the disciples gave to Jesus' question about who he was.

Summary

You should now know about the conversation at Caesarea Philippi and its importance.

> **"** Six days later, Jesus took with him Peter and James and John, and led them up a high mountain apart, by themselves. And he was transfigured before them, and his clothes became dazzling white, such as no one on earth could bleach them. And there appeared to them Elijah with Moses, who were talking with Jesus. Then Peter said to Jesus, '**Rabbi**, it is good for us to be here; let us make three dwellings, one for you, one for Moses, and one for Elijah.' He did not know what to say, for they were terrified. Then a cloud overshadowed them, and from the cloud there came a voice, 'This is my Son, the Beloved; listen to him!' Suddenly when they looked around, they saw no one with them any more, but only Jesus. As they were coming down the mountain, he ordered them to tell no one about what they had seen, until after the Son of Man had risen from the dead. **"**
>
> *Mark 9:2–9* [NRSV]

Objective

- Learn about the **transfiguration** of Jesus and understand the importance of the event to believers.

Key terms

- **transfiguration:** the event in Mark's Gospel where Jesus' clothes are described as glowing dazzling white
- **Rabbi:** a Jewish teacher
- **mystical experience:** a religious event where people see and feel things that create a sense of awe and fascination

Research activity

Read about the time when the Jews left Egypt and the giving of the Ten Commandments in Exodus 19 and 20.

This incident follows the conversation in Caesarea Philippi in which Peter recognised Jesus as the Messiah (Christ). On this occasion Jesus had with him only Peter, James and John, just as he had when he brought Jairus' daughter back to life.

■ Jesus' transformation

Mark describes how the disciples saw Jesus' appearance change and his clothes became 'dazzling white'. In Jewish tradition such brightness was associated with the 'Shekinah' – the presence of God. Mark's description of this event shows how the disciples came to see that Jesus was the Son of God.

■ The presence of Elijah and Moses

Elijah represented the prophets and Moses represented the Law. The Hebrew Scriptures (Old Testament) are divided into three parts in Judaism: the Law (Torah), the Prophets (Nevi'im) and the Writings (Ketuvim). Christians believe that this event shows that Jesus was fulfilling God's promises, given to the Jews in the Law and the Prophets. The fact that Jesus is linked to Moses, the leader of the Jews at the time of the Exodus, demonstrates that he too would bring about salvation.

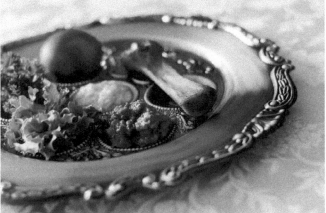

▲ *Jews today celebrate during the festival of Passover the time when Moses won his people's freedom from slavery*

■ Moses

Moses was the means of God's salvation, rescuing the Jews from slavery, and leading them after they left Egypt. He had challenged Pharaoh to let the people go and, when Pharaoh refused, there had been ten plagues to emphasise that Moses was speaking with God's authority.

During the next 40 years, as the Jews wandered through the desert, Moses was in communication with God. He received from God the Ten Commandments and other laws so that the Jews, in keeping them, would remain close to God. The Ten Commandments became the basis of the Law (Torah).

■ Elijah

Elijah was a prophet in the ninth century BCE. He lived much of his life in danger, but this did not stop him prophesying. He spoke fearlessly against injustice and in support of people following their religion properly. He was prepared to challenge all who failed in this. The Jews believe that Elijah will reappear before the Messiah comes.

■ The voice from heaven

Mark describes how a voice came from above, just as it had at Jesus' baptism. This voice is also assumed to be God, telling the disciples that this is his Son, whom he loves, and they are to listen to Jesus. These words indicated to the disciples the authority Jesus had as Son of God.

■ The disciples' reaction

The disciples were afraid. Again, it was Peter who spoke first. He offered to put up three shelters for Jesus, Elijah and Moses. In the time of Moses, in the desert, the people had a special tent or shelter used for prayer and Peter may have remembered this when he saw the transfiguration and heard the voice.

■ The importance of the transfiguration for Christians

Notice in this passage how, even after this event, Jesus still asks the disciples to keep the Messianic Secret. The tone of the Gospel changes after the events at Caesarea Philippi. The early Christians believed (as Christians do today) that the transfiguration was an important event because it shows Jesus as Son of God. Peter's offer to build shelters shows that he recognised that he was in the presence of God. In the time of Mark, when Christians were being persecuted by the Jewish and Roman communities, the account of the transfiguration might have been important in convincing Jews that Christians were not rejecting the message of the Old Testament, and were not a threat to Jewish beliefs. Some Christians today still keep a special day for remembering the transfiguration on 6 August. It reminds them that Jesus was both man and God at the same time.

■ Explanations of the transfiguration

For Christians the transfiguration is a **mystical experience** that defies scientific explanation. However, a number of other explanations have been put forward, including:

- The disciples had a vision or a dream
- It actually happened after the resurrection of Jesus, but has been put into the Gospel at an earlier time to strengthen the belief that Jesus is the Son of God.

▲ *The Basilica of the Transfiguration in Galilee, Israel, built on Mount Tabor, believed to be the place where transfiguration took place*

⭐ Study tip

It is important that you do not muddle the two incidents of the baptism and the transfiguration.

The passion prediction of Jesus – Mark 10:32–34

> **❝** They were on the road, going up to Jerusalem, and Jesus was walking ahead of them; they were amazed, and those who followed were afraid. He took the Twelve aside again and began to tell them what was to happen to him, saying, 'See, we are going up to Jerusalem, and the Son of Man will be handed over to the chief priests and the scribes, and they will condemn him to death; then they will hand him over to the Gentiles; they will mock him, and spit upon him, and flog him, and kill him; and after three days he will rise.' **❞**
>
> *Mark* 10:32–34 [NRSV]

Objective

● Understand the passion predictions of Jesus.

Key term

● **Gentile:** someone who is not Jewish

■ Jesus' passion prediction

According to the passion predictions, Jesus knew he would face suffering and death as part of his ministry. It was important that the disciples realised this, and that they understood the promise of resurrection at the end of each prediction. His reference to the 'Son of Man' here would have left the disciples in no doubt that he meant himself. In this prediction Jesus confirms that he believes the Messiah will suffer, and that this suffering will lead to his death. He predicts that he will be handed over to the chief priests and scribes.

▲ *Jesus was arrested in the Garden of Gethsemane and his predictions of the following events came true*

Notice that in this prediction Jesus refers to the **Gentiles** who are, in this case, the Romans. The Romans would not have felt threatened by Jesus' religious teachings or claims. They would only respond to him if they felt he threatened their power in the region. People of the time might have assumed Jesus faced a threat from the Jews, who could have accused him of blasphemy. However, this passage shows that Jesus may have known it was the Romans who would threaten his life, because only the Romans could impose the death penalty.

There are two other passion predictions recorded by Mark that are very similar to the one in 10:32–34. The first of these comes after the conversation at Caesarea Philippi (Mark 8:31) and the second after the transfiguration:

> **❝** For he was teaching his disciples, saying to them, 'The Son of Man is to be betrayed into human hands, and they will kill him; and three days after being killed, he will rise again.' But they did not understand what he was saying and were afraid to ask him. **❞**
>
> *Mark* 9:31–32 [NRSV]

Research activity

Find out about the importance of Jerusalem as the capital of Palestine in the first century CE and how it was the religious and political centre of power.

The reactions of the disciples and followers

According to Mark, some of Jesus' followers were 'afraid' at this stage – possibly at the prospect of going to Jerusalem. They may have been aware how dangerous it was for Jesus to go to the religious and political capital and teach there. Mark also records that the disciples were 'amazed', possibly at the power and authority which Jesus showed in his teaching. Amazement and surprise is quite a common occurrence in Mark's Gospel – the crowds were frequently amazed by Jesus' teachings and actions.

▲ *The road to Jerusalem*

Discipleship

Christians can learn about discipleship from the passion prediction. They can see the example that Jesus set and try to follow it.

Commitment

Jesus could have stayed in Galilee, where he was safe, but he did not. His message had to be taken to Jerusalem, even if it meant that he would die. On this occasion, he is described as walking ahead of his followers – perhaps to show his determination to go through with his plan. Christians understand from this that they sometimes need to be determined to do what they know is right, even if it is difficult.

Suffering

The disciples did not realise it at the time, but they too would almost all die a martyr's death for their beliefs. Christians believe they need to be prepared to face suffering and to make sacrifices if necessary to remain true to their faith.

Links

See pages 24–25 to read Jesus' passion prediction in Mark 8:31.

Extension activity

Find out why some people think that the passion predictions were not historical but were added after the events of Jesus' death and resurrection.

Activities

1 Explain why you think the disciples did not understand Jesus' teaching about his suffering and death, and what made them afraid.

2 'If Jesus had stayed away from Jerusalem he would not have had to die as he did.' Evaluate this statement. Try to give reasoned arguments for more than one point of view.

3 Read the passage in Isaiah 53 about the suffering servant. Draw a table with two columns. In one column, list all the things that happened to the suffering servant and, in the other, as you read Mark's Gospel, add the things that happened to Jesus after his arrest.

⭐ **Study tip**

Learn the passion prediction in detail because knowing it will assist in understanding what happened to Jesus at the end of his life.

Summary

You should now understand Jesus' prediction of what would happen to him in Jerusalem.

The request of James and John – Mark 10:35–45

> 66 James and John, the sons of Zebedee, came forward to him, and said to him, 'Teacher, we want you to do for us whatever we ask of you.' And he said to them, 'What is it you want me to do for you?' And they said to him, 'Grant us to sit, one at your right hand and one at your left, in your glory.' But Jesus said to them, 'You do not know what you are asking. Are you able to drink the cup that I drink, or be baptised with the baptism that I am baptised with?' They replied, 'We are able.' Then Jesus said to them, 'The cup that I drink you will drink; and with the baptism with which I am baptised, you will be baptised; but to sit at my right hand or at my left is not mine to grant, but it is for those for whom it has been prepared.'
>
> When the ten heard this, they began to be angry with James and John. So Jesus called them and said to them, 'You know that among the Gentiles those whom they recognise as their rulers lord it over them, and their great ones are tyrants over them. But it is not so among you; but whoever wishes to become great among you must be your servant, and whoever wishes to be first among you must be slave of all. For the Son of Man came not to be served but to serve, and to give his life [as] a **ransom** for many.' 99
>
> *Mark* 10:35–45 [NRSV]

Objective

- Learn about the request of James and John and understand Jesus' answer to them.

Key terms

- **ransom:** usually a payment made to release a hostage; in Roman times, a payment made to get someone out of prison
- **vocation:** feeling called by God to undertake an action, work or to follow a particular career

This is an occasion on which the disciples are shown to be slow to grasp Jesus' message, and also to have very human failings. The question may suggest that James and John had not understood the nature of the sacrifice that Jesus was going to make. By this point he had made three passion predictions, but according to Mark these disciples were only interested in their own glory. Nevertheless, their question does show that they understood that Jesus would one day be in 'glory' – this means life after death. They understood Jesus' special relationship with God.

◼ Jesus' answer

Mark describes how Jesus asked the two disciples what they wanted him to do for them. He then explained to them that they did not understand what they were asking. On many occasions Jesus answered a question with another question.

In the Old Testament, the cup often signified something given by God (Isaiah 51:17 and Psalm 23:5 are good examples). In this passage the cup represents whatever is given to a person in their life – their destiny. According to Mark, later in the Gospel Jesus also used the image of a cup in Gethsemane, where he asked for the 'cup' to be taken away from him (Mark 14:36).

The reference to baptism here emphasises Jesus' humanity. He had previously shown that he identified with sinners, so this could be a reference to him taking on all the sins of humanity. In asking the

Activities

1 Describe what Christians could sacrifice for their faith.

2 'Serving the Church is the most important thing a Christian does.' What do you think? Give reasons for your answer.

brothers whether they were prepared to face the same experiences as he did, in order to sit on his right and left in heaven, Jesus was warning them how difficult it could be to be a disciple.

■ Suffering and discipleship

Mark explains that the brothers told Jesus they believed they were 'able' to follow him, even if it meant suffering and death. Indeed, this turned out to be true. The disciples were persecuted and did suffer at the hands of the Romans. James was executed by Herod Agrippa, the Jewish King, according to Christian tradition. John was more fortunate: he escaped from persecution and ended his life in exile in Ephesus.

The anger expressed here by the other disciples enabled Jesus to teach them about authority and leadership. As Mark describes, Jesus explained that the disciples must not seek power and authority, but instead serve. Jesus was teaching something that his hearers would have been surprised by: anyone who wants to be a leader must be a slave to others. In those days, a slave was lower than a servant, so Jesus' comments would have had a very dramatic effect.

Jesus' apparent description of his death as 'ransom' suggests that he understood the price he would pay for the sin of all people. In Hebrew, the word for ransom means to 'cover over', so Jesus appears to have said that he will either 'bail people out of sin' or 'cover their sins'. Either way, Mark is telling readers that Jesus taught his disciples to focus on helping other people, rather than seeking the best places in heaven.

■ Christian understanding of this incident today

Many Christians who read Mark 10: 35–45 understand that sometimes in prayer, they ask for things which are selfish. When prayers seem to be unanswered, or those who pray do not get the answer they desire, Christians might question the power of prayer. The brothers here did not get the answer they wanted – Christianity teaches that perhaps they were asking for the wrong thing.

Many Christians make sacrifices or perform acts of service for the Church. One example is the tradition of priests washing believers' feet on Maundy Thursday. Another example comes from nuns and monks, who make vows of poverty, chastity and obedience. Some religious leaders will not marry so that they can devote their whole life to the service of the Church. Some Christians have vocations in which they believe they can serve others, such as working in teaching, the police force or the health service.

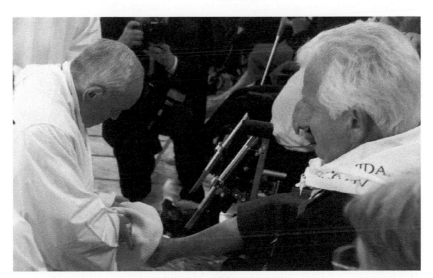

▲ *Church leaders today still perform acts of service; here Pope Francis washes believers' feet as part of the worship on Maundy Thursday*

Summary

You should now have a knowledge of the incident of James and John's request and understand Jesus' teaching that Christian discipleship means service.

> 66 They came to Jericho. As he and his disciples and a large crowd were leaving Jericho, Bartimaeus son of Timaeus, a blind beggar, was sitting by the roadside. When he heard that it was Jesus of Nazareth, he began to shout out and say, 'Jesus, Son of David, have mercy on me!' Many sternly ordered him to be quiet; but he cried out even more loudly, 'Son of David, have mercy on me!' Jesus stood still and said, 'Call him here.' And they called the blind man, saying to him, 'Take heart; get up, he is calling you.' So throwing off his cloak, he sprang up and came to Jesus. Then Jesus said to him, 'What do you want me to do for you?' The blind man said to him, 'My teacher, let me see again.' Jesus said to him, 'Go; your faith has made you well.' Immediately he regained his sight and followed him on the way. 99
>
> *Mark* 10:46–52 [NRSV]

Jericho is near the Dead Sea. It is the first place that the Hebrews settled after years wandering in the desert, following their escape from Egypt.

■ Bartimaeus

The name Bartimaeus is Aramaic – the common language in Israel at this time. Mark explains to the reader that it means 'son of Timaeus' (a clue that the Gospel was written outside Israel, or was written for a non-Jewish audience). The significance of the miracle is that Bartimaeus, even though he was blind, could see that Jesus was the Messiah better than the crowds gathered around him.

Mark describes how Bartimaeus used the title 'Son of David'. This might have been dangerous, so this may be part of the reason the crowd told Bartimaeus to be quiet. Notice that Bartimaeus was apparently sitting 'by the roadside' when he called out. This means that he was regarded as an outsider. The disabled were often regarded as unclean in some way, because many at the time believed that their disability was caused by sin, either their sin or a sin that their parents had committed. For this reason Bartimaeus would not have been allowed in the Temple.

According to Mark, Bartimaeus abandoned his cloak. At that time the outer garment would have been very important. In this instance it was probably spread on the ground to catch any money given. According to Mark, Bartimaeus was so anxious to meet Jesus that he left what little he had. There is a parallel here between the behaviour of Bartimaeus and the reaction to Jesus of the first disciples. In that case Mark describes how they also left everything they had (Mark 1:18, 20). Like Bartimaeus, their lives were transformed.

Objective

● Study the account of the healing of Bartimaeus and understand its meaning for the disciples and for Christians today.

Activities

1 What did Bartimaeus do which demonstrated his faith?

2 What clues are there in this narrative to indicate that it was written for, and would be read by, Gentiles?

▲ *Jesus heals Bartimaeus*

After the healing, Mark writes that Bartimaeus followed Jesus on the road. He had apparently not only been healed, but had been brought back into society, possibly to become a follower and disciple (though he was not one of the twelve).

▲ *A photo of modern day Jericho*

■ Jesus and his actions

Jesus asked Bartimaeus what he wanted. Bartimaeus wanted his health restored; he wanted to see again (unlike James and John who wanted power and status).

Jesus could have just healed Bartimaeus and gone on, but according to Mark he did not. Jesus drew attention to the fact that it was Bartimaeus' faith that had enabled him to regain his sight, which was to be a lesson for the crowd.

■ Christian understanding of this incident today

For Christian believers today there is a challenge posed by this story. Jesus was happy to help someone who was regarded as an outsider and ignored. Christians today are faced with similar problems – the need to help those who have been rejected by society.

Christians helping less-fortunate people

Betel is a Christian organisation that was founded in Spain in 1985. Its first UK centre was opened in 1996. Betel UK is dedicated to restoring homeless, addicted and long-term unemployed people to healthy, independent lifestyles. They offer a home to about 350 recovering people. Training in life skills and employment preparation helps residents to rebuild their lives. They state, 'Betel's mission is to bring long-term freedom and restoration to lives broken by drug and alcohol abuse. We accomplish this by building values, skills and character through living, working and worshipping together in a caring Christian community.'

(www.betel.uk)

Activity

1 What do Jesus' words and actions teach about his relationship with God?

Extension activity

Read Mark 8:22–26, about the healing of another blind man.

⭐ Study tip

Try to explain how this account of Christian healing is important to the Christian faith today

Summary
You should now have an example of a healing in which faith played a central role.

> **"** When they were approaching Jerusalem, at Bethphage and Bethany, near the Mount of Olives, he sent two of his disciples, and said to them, 'Go into the village ahead of you, and immediately as you enter it, you will find tied there a colt that has never been ridden; untie it and bring it. If anyone says to you, "Why are you doing this?" just say this, "The Lord needs it and will send it back here immediately."' They went away and found a colt tied near a door, outside in the street. As they were untying it some of the bystanders said to them, 'What are you doing, untying the colt?' They told them what Jesus had said; and they allowed them to take it. Then they brought the colt to Jesus and threw their cloaks on it; and he sat on it. Many people spread their cloaks on the road, and others spread leafy branches that they had cut in the fields. Then those who went ahead and those who followed were shouting,
>
> 'Hosanna!
>
> Blessed is the one who comes in the name of the Lord!
>
> Blessed is the coming Kingdom of our ancestor David!
>
> Hosanna in the highest heaven!'
>
> Then he entered Jerusalem and went into the Temple; and when he had looked around at everything, as it was already late, he went out to Bethany with the Twelve. **"**
>
> *Mark* 11:1–11 [NRSV]

Objective

● Learn about and understand the significance of the entry of Jesus into Jerusalem.

Key term

● **passion narrative:** the part of Mark's Gospel which deals with the last week of Jesus' life and his suffering

▲ *A palm cross; people spread leafy branches or palms before Jesus and Christians use these crosses made from palm leaves*

This is the beginning of the **passion narrative** – the story of the last week of Jesus' life – in Mark's Gospel. This passage is sometimes called the 'Triumphal Entry', because it describes how the people responded as if a king or great ruler had arrived, placing palm branches on the road in front of Jesus. Bethany, about two miles from the centre of Jerusalem, seems to have been the place where Jesus based himself during this time. Mark writes that the disciples were given an instruction, which they followed. It seems strange that they could just take a colt without checking with the owner first. Perhaps an arrangement with the owner had been made earlier.

It is important to note that it was nearly Passover and there would have been many pilgrims from all over the Middle East in Jerusalem. It would be a time when the Romans were very suspicious of the Jewish crowds and anticipated trouble. They would have been aware of the greeting that Jesus was given, although they may not have fully understood the symbolism of it. It is not clear how many people greeted Jesus – it may just have been those who had travelled with him to Jerusalem from Jericho.

Activities

1 Describe, in your own words, what the disciples might have thought about Jesus' entry into Jerusalem.

2 Do you think Jesus deliberately chose to enter Jerusalem to act out the prophecy of Zechariah? Why?

Research activity

Look up Zechariah 9:9; 2 Kings 9:13 and Psalm 118:26. How do these three Old Testament references help to understand Jesus' entry into Jerusalem?

The Mount of Olives

The Mount of Olives has been a place of worship since King David captured Jerusalem (2 Samuel 15:32), and is important in Jewish tradition. In the book of Zechariah (14:4), the Mount of Olives is given as the place where the final judgement will take place.

The colt

The word for a colt in Greek could mean a young horse or a donkey. It is more likely in this instance that it was the latter. According to Mark, when the disciples were questioned about the taking of the colt, they replied that 'the Lord' needed it. The word 'Lord' can mean 'God', but in this instance it means 'the master'.

The significance of the colt is that it was not a horse that a warrior would ride. In the Old Testament the Messiah is referred to as riding a colt (Zechariah 9:9). Mark suggests a messianic role for Jesus here, and also a kingly role. However, the difference between the traditional view of the Messiah king and this description of Jesus is that Jesus was, according to Mark, portraying himself as a peaceful Messiah who was not a warrior king. This was considered a sign that he was not likely to take up arms against the Romans.

The reaction of the people

Mark describes how the people spread cloaks and branches on the road as a mark that they believed the king had come. The shouting of 'hosanna' is important. The word 'hosanna' in Hebrew literally means 'save I pray', so the people apparently wanted Jesus to save them. The crowd then referred to the coming Kingdom of David and clearly believed Jesus was the Messiah (Christ).

The significance of the entry into Jerusalem for Christians

Christians today remember the entry of Jesus into Jerusalem on Palm Sunday, the Sunday before Easter Day. On that day they often receive palm crosses at the Sunday church service. The service begins the special Holy Week in which Christians remember the events that led up to Jesus' crucifixion and resurrection. Christians today walk from place to place as a witness, they carry palms and crosses, and there are special services. Christians believe that when Jesus entered Jerusalem on a donkey, he showed his humility and his desire for peace.

⭐ **Study tip**

Remember, this account is crucial in understanding Jesus as a peaceful Messiah.

> ❝ Rejoice greatly,
> O daughter Zion!
>
> Shout aloud, O daughter Jerusalem!
>
> Lo, your king comes to you,
>
> triumphant and victorious is he,
>
> humble and riding on a donkey,
>
> on a colt, the foal of a donkey. ❞
>
> *Zechariah* 9:9 [NRSV]

▲ *Christians in India taking part in a Palm Sunday procession*

Summary

You should now understand the importance of the entry of Jesus into Jerusalem and its significance for Christians today.

3 The final days in Jerusalem

3.1 The Last Supper – Mark 14:12–26

> On the first day of Unleavened Bread, when the **Passover** lamb is sacrificed, his disciples said to him, 'Where do you want us to go and make the preparations for you to eat the Passover?' So he sent two of his disciples, saying to them, 'Go into the city, and a man carrying a jar of water will meet you; follow him, and wherever he enters, say to the owner of the house, "The Teacher asks, Where is my guest room, where I may eat the Passover with my disciples?" He will show you a large room upstairs, furnished and ready. Make preparations for us there.' So the disciples set out and went to the city, and found everything as he had told them; and they prepared the Passover meal.
>
> When it was evening, he came with the Twelve. And when they had taken their places and were eating, Jesus said, 'Truly I tell you, one of you will betray me, one who is eating with me.' They began to be distressed and to say to him one after another, 'Surely, not I?' He said to them, 'It is one of the Twelve, one who is dipping bread into the bowl with me. For the Son of Man goes as it is written of him, but woe to that one by whom the Son of Man is betrayed! It would have been better for that one not to have been born.'
>
> While they were eating, he took a loaf of bread, and after blessing it he broke it, gave it to them, and said, 'Take; this is my body.' Then he took a cup, and after giving thanks he gave it to them, and all of them drank from it. He said to them, 'This is my blood of the **covenant**, which is poured out for many. Truly I tell you, I will never again drink of the fruit of the vine until that day when I drink it new in the **Kingdom of God**.'
>
> When they had sung the hymn, they went out to the Mount of Olives.
>
> *Mark* 14:12–26 [NRSV]

Key terms

- **Passover:** the Jewish festival held in the spring which commemorates the freeing of the Hebrew slaves from Egypt
- **covenant:** the agreement between God and the Jews that he would be their God and they would be his people
- **Kingdom of God:** in the teaching of Jesus: 1. the reign of God on earth now 2. heaven, the afterlife
- **Holy Communion:** the giving of bread and wine as a memorial of Jesus in church services; also referred to as Eucharist (thanksgiving), Mass or The Lord's Supper
- **transubstantiation:** the belief that at the consecration, the bread and wine actually become the body and blood of Christ

Mark's Gospel states that the Last Supper was a Passover meal. Jesus planned to eat one last meal with the disciples, although the disciples didn't know that it was to be their last meal together. The sharing of such a meal was a sign of community and it should have been a joyous occasion, as Jesus and his disciples ate and drank together in celebration.

■ The disciples' preparation

Traditionally it is thought that the Last Supper was held in John Mark's mother's house in Jerusalem. The disciples had to look for a man carrying water. This would have been unusual, since in those days fetching and carrying water was a woman's task.

Activities

1 Explain carefully the meaning of the bread and the wine in Holy Communion.

2 How does celebrating Holy Communion give Christians a sense of community?

■ Jesus' words

Jesus knew that the easiest way for the authorities to arrest him was to find him when he was not surrounded by crowds of people. This would mean one of the group betraying him and informing the authorities where he would be.

Mark's Gospel gives us no clue at this stage, but we do know that it was Judas Iscariot who informed the authorities. According to Mark, Jesus said that it would be better for the betrayer that he had not been born.

■ Jesus' actions

Breaking bread and drinking wine are normal parts of the Passover meal, but Jesus gave these actions new meaning for his followers. Mark describes how Jesus took the bread, gave thanks and broke it. Breaking bread to share with others was a Jewish mealtime tradition. Bread is blessed at every Sabbath evening meal in many Jewish homes.

In this passage Mark also describe how Jesus said the broken bread was his body. It shows that Jesus' body would be 'broken' and that he would be seriously injured and die.

According to Mark, Jesus then took the cup of wine, ready to share it with the disciples. Jesus highlighted the importance of the wine and its connection with the covenant. This is the agreement that Jews believe God made with them – that he would be their God and they would be his people (Genesis 17). Jesus was here describing a new covenant between God and his people, and the disciples were to be part of this new agreement. Through Jesus' life and death, people would be able to approach God and live a life close to God. The reference to Jesus not drinking wine again until he reached the Kingdom of God was a reminder of his imminent death, as well as the arrival of the Kingdom of God, which the early Church believed would take place soon.

■ The importance of the Last Supper to Christians

In the early Church, one of the important parts of worship was the communal meal or 'the Lord's Supper'. In Paul's letters, he gave the Christians instructions on how this should be done, using many of Jesus' original words (I Corinthians 11:23–26).

Many churches still remember the Last Supper in the service of Holy Communion. They use bread and wine and repeat the words of Jesus. (I Corinthians 11:23–26). It reminds them of the sacrifice Jesus made. Catholics believe the bread and wine actually become the body and blood of Jesus (called transubstantiation), whereas the Protestant tradition teaches that the bread and wine are symbols of Jesus' body and blood. Catholics and Anglicans celebrate Holy Communion every week. Non-conformist churches may hold Communion services once or twice a month. The Salvation Army and Quakers (Society of Friends) do not celebrate Holy Communion, believing that any kind of ritual is unnecessary for faith.

▲ *The Last Supper is often a subject for artists*

Extension activity

Early Christians, persecuted by the Romans, were accused of 'cannibalism'. Using your knowledge of the Last Supper and Christian worship, explain how this could have been believed.

Research activities

1   Look up what happens at the Jewish Passover. Explain how Jesus may be compared with the Passover lamb.

2   To see a modern Passover meal, search 'Passover Seder' on YouTube.

⭐ **Study tip**

It is important to learn and remember both Jesus' words and his actions in this story.

Summary

You should now have an understanding of the importance of the Last Supper for Jesus and the disciples and for Christians, both in the early church and today.

Objective

- Study the events in Gethsemane at the time of the arrest of Jesus.

Activities

1 Should Jesus have avoided going to the Garden of Gethsemane and being arrested? Explain your answer.

2 Why do you think Jesus was arrested as a rebel?

3 Why did Jesus accept his arrest?

4 Jesus said, 'let the scriptures be fulfilled'. Look again at Isaiah 50:6 and 53, and see what is predicted there.

> ❝ They went to a place called Gethsemane; and he said to his disciples, 'Sit here while I pray.' He took with him Peter and James and John, and began to be distressed and agitated. And he said to them, 'I am deeply grieved, even to death; remain here, and keep awake.' And going a little farther, he threw himself on the ground and prayed that, if it were possible, the hour might pass from him. He said, 'Abba, Father, for you all things are possible; remove this cup from me; yet, not what I want, but what you want.' He came and found them sleeping; and he said to Peter, 'Simon, are you asleep? Could you not keep awake one hour? Keep awake and pray that you may not come into the time of trial; the spirit indeed is willing, but the flesh is weak.' And again he went away and prayed, saying the same words. And once more he came and found them sleeping, for their eyes were very heavy; and they did not know what to say to him. He came a third time and said to them, 'Are you still sleeping and taking your rest? Enough! The hour has come; the Son of Man is betrayed into the hands of sinners. Get up, let us be going. See, my betrayer is at hand.'
>
> Immediately, while he was still speaking, Judas, one of the Twelve, arrived; and with him there was a crowd with swords and clubs, from the chief priests, the scribes, and the elders. Now the betrayer had given them a sign, saying, 'The one I will kiss is the man; arrest him and lead him away under guard.' So when he came, he went up to him at once and said, 'Rabbi!' and kissed him. Then they laid hands on him and arrested him. But one of those who stood near drew his sword, and struck the slave of the high priest, cutting off his ear. Then Jesus said to them, 'Have you come out with swords and clubs to arrest me as though I were a bandit? Day after day I was with you in the temple teaching, and you did not arrest me. But let the scriptures be fulfilled.' All of them deserted him and fled.
>
> A certain young man was following him, wearing nothing but a linen cloth. They caught hold of him, but he left the linen cloth and ran off naked. ❞
>
> *Mark* 14:32–52 [NRSV]

The Garden of Gethsemane was an olive grove that was out of the city. After the Last Supper, Jesus and the disciples went there. The events of the night indicate the turmoil of the last hours of Jesus' life. Mark usually stresses Jesus' authority, but on this occasion Jesus is depicted as vulnerable and isolated.

■ Jesus' prayer

Jesus' prayer in this passage was a plea for God to save him, or take the 'cup' from him. He was asking God to spare him the suffering he was going to face. The word Jesus used for God was the Aramaic 'Abba', which means 'father'. This shows the closeness that Jesus had to God, his father. Jesus accepted that God's will should be done. This prayer

▲ *A statue depicting Jesus' arrest; Jesus submitted peacefully to his arrest*

would have inspired the early Christians facing persecution. If Jesus was prepared to do God's will, even when it would lead to his own suffering, then they should also accept the will of God.

■ The disciples

This is one of the occasions when it could be argued that the disciples let Jesus down. Three times Jesus came back from praying to find them sleeping. This is not so surprising, given that it was late – they may well have been weary. They would also have been anxious about their presence in Jerusalem, about the growing opposition to Jesus and about Jesus' indications that he was about to suffer.

Jesus warned them that they should not fall into the 'time of trial'. Jesus would have been reminded of his time in the desert and the rebuke he had given Peter at Caesarea Philippi. It can also mean testing and Jesus was telling them to pray that they would not be tested, as Jesus was about to be.

■ The arrest

Judas led a group of Temple police and others to arrest Jesus. The familiar kiss contrasts starkly with Judas' true intention – to identify Jesus to his captors. Throughout history Judas has been described as the 'betrayer'. His name 'Iscariot' could mean either a 'man of Kerioth' (a village in modern-day Israel) or 'a member of the sicarii'. The sicarii were Zealots who were opposed to the Romans and carried a small dagger called a sica. They used this to attack political enemies. If Judas was a Zealot, then he may have thought that Jesus was a political messiah. He may have thought that creating a confrontation with the authorities would inspire Jesus to tell his followers to begin the battle against the Romans. However, if this was his thinking, Judas was wrong.

The disciples were prepared to assist Jesus. Indeed one of them cut off the ear of the high priest's servant. The disciple is not named in Mark's Gospel but John's Gospel names Peter as the disciple who struck the servant (John 18: 10). This violent response was not what Jesus wanted. He was a peaceful teacher who wanted justice.

Jesus noted that he had taught in the Temple but had not been arrested. This is not surprising. It is estimated that there could have been an additional 26,000 pilgrims in the Temple during Passover. There could have been a riot had Jesus been arrested there. Jesus said 'let the scriptures be fulfilled' and submitted to being taken to suffer and die (just as predicted in Isaiah 53).

The disciples, who had followed Jesus faithfully for three years, were frightened and ran away.

■ The young man

Some believe that the young man who ran away naked was John Mark – the assumed author of Mark's Gospel. The presence of this 'young man' is not mentioned in any other gospel. If the Last Supper had been at his mother's house, then he could have followed them to the garden. It is one of the indicators that Mark's Gospel could include eyewitness testimony.

Links

See pages 30–31 to read about Jesus telling James and John that they must drink from the same cup as him.

▲ *In the Church of All Nations in the Garden of Gethsemane, there is a rock where Jesus is said to have prayed.*

⭐ **Study tip**

Ensure that you know in detail what took place in Gethsemane, especially Jesus' prayer.

Summary

You should now know and understand the events surrounding Jesus' arrest.

> ❝ They took Jesus to the high priest; and all the chief priests, the elders, and the scribes were assembled … Some stood up and gave false testimony against him, saying, 'We heard him say, "I will destroy this temple that is made with hands, and in three days I will build another, not made with hands."' But even on this point their testimony did not agree.
>
> Then the high priest stood up before them and asked Jesus, 'Have you no answer? What is it that they testify against you?' But he was silent and did not answer. Again the high priest asked him, 'Are you the Messiah, the Son of the Blessed One?' Jesus said, 'I am; and 'you will see the Son of Man seated at the right hand of the Power', and 'coming with the clouds of heaven.'
>
> Then the high priest tore his clothes and said, 'Why do we still need witnesses? You have heard his **blasphemy**. What is your decision?' All of them condemned him as deserving death. Some began to spit on him, and to blindfold, and to strike him, saying to him, 'Prophesy!' The guards also took him over and beat him. ❞
>
> *Mark* 14:53, 57–65 [NRSV]

Objective

- Learn about and understand the trial of Jesus before the Jewish authorities.

Key terms

- **blasphemy:** a religious offence that includes claiming to be God
- **Sanhedrin:** the Jewish Council at the time of Jesus; it consisted of 71 members, met in Jerusalem and was led by the High Priest

■ The Jewish leaders

The Jewish leaders had come to a special agreement with the Romans. The Roman authorities allowed them to follow their own religion. They were not required to worship the Emperor, and Roman coins in Palestine did not usually have the Emperor's head on them. It was a delicate balance of power. The Jewish leaders did not want this upset by the hints of political unrest that had come with Jesus' presence in Jerusalem. They may also have disliked his teaching, because he opposed the religious authorities and challenged religious practice.

The **Sanhedrin** was a council that consisted of the powerful Jews in Israel – the High Priest and chief priests, Sadducees, scribes and Pharisees. It included teachers, priests and lawyers. The Jewish rules of justice were broken in Jesus' trial. The Sanhedrin was not allowed to pass the death sentence, nor was it allowed to try suspects at night. Mark does not indicate whether it was day or night, but we can assume it was night because this was straight after Jesus' arrest. (Luke says it was daybreak.) There were also supposed to be a minimum of 23 members present – not very likely at that time of night. Finally, if there was a call for the death sentence, then a second hearing should have taken place the next day to allow the court to show mercy. No second hearing was held.

▲ *The Church of St Peter in Gallicantu has been built on the site where Jesus was tried; the word Gallicantu refers to a cock's crow (see pages 84–85)*

■ The trial

According to Mark, some people were prepared to lie to the court to ensure that Jesus was convicted. The problem was that their stories did not match. This must have been embarrassing for the Council. Just like the servant in Isaiah 53, Jesus did not answer these false witnesses, but remained silent. So the high priest asked Jesus directly whether he was the Messiah. Under Jewish legal rules he should not have done this, because the accused should not be able to be condemned with their own words.

Jesus' answer was short but dangerous for him. When he said 'I am,' Jesus was echoing the words of God, who told Moses his name was 'I am', which is 'YHWH' in the original Hebrew (Exodus 3:14). To the Council, this answer was blasphemy, because Jesus was claiming to be God. But Jesus went on to use the term 'Son of Man', which they would have interpreted in a messianic way because it suited their case. He then said that he would be seated at the side of 'the Power' (God) and come on the 'clouds of heaven'. This picture of heaven and Jesus coming in power and glory was offensive to the high priest. The reference to the Son of Man here reflects Daniel 7:13:

▲ *Jesus remained silent while the witnesses gave false testimonies*

> **"** As I watched in the night visions,
> I saw one like a human being
> coming with the clouds of heaven.
> And he came to the Ancient One
> and was presented before him. **"**
>
> *Daniel* 7:13 [NRSV]

At his trial, Jesus was claiming the full authority of God, something Mark makes clear right from beginning of his gospel. Saying 'I am' and linking himself to the Son of Man and the heavenly image led to Jesus' conviction.

The tearing of clothes was a sign of rage, and Jesus was convicted of blasphemy. The Old Testament punishment for blasphemy was death by stoning. The Sanhedrin demanded this, even though they did not have the authority to pass a death sentence. Jesus' torture then began. Christians believe it fulfilled the prophecy in Isaiah 50:6: 'I gave my back to those who struck me, and my cheeks to those who pulled out the beard; I did not hide my face from insult and spitting.' [NRSV]

Activities

1 Explain clearly what is meant by blasphemy and why the council charged Jesus with blasphemy.

2 Should Jesus have spoken up in his own defence in this trial?

3 Was the Sanhedrin right to break the rules of the justice system to ensure that Jesus could not challenge them any more?

⭐ Study tip

It is important that you understand that the charge which the Council brought against Jesus here was blasphemy.

Summary

You should now understand the importance of the trial of Jesus before the Jewish authorities and the charge brought against Jesus.

> ❝ As soon as it was morning, the chief priests held a consultation with the elders and scribes and the whole council. They bound Jesus, led him away, and handed him over to Pilate. Pilate asked him, 'Are you the King of the Jews?' He answered him, 'You say so.' Then the chief priests accused him of many things. Pilate asked him again, 'Have you no answer? See how many charges they bring against you.' But Jesus made no further reply, so that Pilate was amazed.
>
> Now at the festival he used to release a prisoner for them, anyone for whom they asked. Now a man called Barabbas was in prison with the rebels who had committed murder during the insurrection. So the crowd came and began to ask Pilate to do for them according to his custom. Then he answered them, 'Do you want me to release for you the King of the Jews?' For he realised that it was out of jealousy that the chief priests had handed him over. But the chief priests stirred up the crowd to have him release Barabbas for them instead. Pilate spoke to them again, 'Then what do you wish me to do with the man you call the King of the Jews?' They shouted back, 'Crucify him!' Pilate asked them, 'Why, what evil has he done?' But they shouted all the more, 'Crucify him!' So Pilate, wishing to satisfy the crowd, released Barabbas for them; and after flogging Jesus, he handed him over to be crucified. ❞
>
> *Mark* 15:1–15 [NRSV]

Objective

- Learn about the trial of Jesus before Pontius Pilate.

Key term

- **martyr:** one who suffers or dies for their belief

Activities

1 'Pilate failed in his duty to uphold justice.' Do you agree? Explain your opinion.

2 Discuss who you think was to blame for Jesus' conviction.

3 Mark seems to show that Pilate did not think Jesus was guilty. Bearing in mind that the Gospel was written at a time of persecution, why might this be important?

4 Explain why Jesus is regarded as a martyr.

Pilate was Governor of the Roman province of Palestine from 26 to 37 CE. A Jewish historian of the period, Josephus, depicted him as harsh and cruel. Philo, another Jewish historian, described him as 'inflexible, stubborn and cruel', and he had the power to sentence people to death. He paid no attention to Jewish feelings when he ordered his troops to enter Jerusalem carrying standards with the image of the Emperor on them. When the crowd protested at this, Pilate eventually ordered the images to be removed.

■ Pilate's role

Pilate had a duty to uphold Roman justice. Yet he was faced with a problem when the Sanhedrin brought Jesus to him. Either he could uphold justice and let Jesus go free, or he could give in to the crowd and avoid a riot. If he gave in to the Jews, he knew that he would probably be condemning an innocent man to death.

Pilate was not interested in blasphemy, so claims about the Messiah or the name of God had no effect on him. However, according to Mark he asked Jesus whether he was a king. This had political implications; Jesus could be sentenced to death for treason by claiming to be a king. As Jesus avoided giving a direct answer, Pilate then prompted Jesus to give a full response. Jesus gave no further answer, and Pilate, like the

▲ *Pontius Pilate depicted in a stained glass window at St Lawrence Church in Essex; Pilate had to deal with many rebellions during his governorship and he was known for being ruthless with the rebels*

crowds elsewhere in Mark's Gospel, was amazed. According to Mark, Pilate was amazed by Jesus' lack of response. Mark elsewhere in his gospel describes how Jesus amazed people who saw him.

Pilate then asked the crowd what they wanted. The people called for Jesus to be crucified. They did not want Pilate to release the 'King of the Jews'. When he asked them what wrong Jesus had committed, the crowd could not answer because Jesus had broken no Roman laws. They just shouted louder, 'Crucify him!'

Mark notes how Pilate knew that the Sanhedrin had brought Jesus out of jealousy. However, Barabbas was released and Jesus handed over to be flogged and crucified.

Flogging was extremely cruel. There was no limit to the number of lashes that could be given. In some cases it was so severe that the prisoner died before crucifixion. It was thought that it shortened the length of time criminals were on the cross.

▲ *A 16th-century painting of Jesus appearing before Pontius Pilate; as a Roman Governor, Pilate wanted to charge Jesus for a political crime – treason – rather than the religious one – blasphemy*

■ Barabbas

Barabbas is described by Mark as a rebel imprisoned following the uprising. It is not clear which uprising, but it seems there was a strong case to convict him of treason. He may well have been one of the members of the Zealot groups in Jerusalem. There are no records of prisoners being released at Passover, but if Pilate was trying to calm down the crowd, it is not unlikely that he would release a prisoner.

■ Jesus' conviction

Who was to blame for Jesus' wrongful conviction?

* Judas had handed Jesus over to the authorities. Had he misjudged what was going to happen?
* The members of the Sanhedrin were determined to get Jesus sentenced to death. They believed he was guilty of blasphemy, and they deliberately changed the charge to treason to ensure he was sentenced to death.
* Pilate had a responsibility as a Roman Governor to uphold justice. Yet he gave in to the crowds and the Jewish leaders and sentenced an innocent man to death.
* Jesus could have defended himself. He said very little to Pilate. However, he knew that God had a plan for him. He came from a tradition in which salvation – that is being able to approach God – came from the blood sacrifice of an animal. Jesus could have believed that his death was part of God's plan and that he had to die. He could also have regarded himself as a **martyr**. Had Jesus decided not to go to Gethsemane, he might not have been arrested.
* The crowd shouted for Jesus' death, but were encouraged to do so by their leaders.

Extension activity

Use the Internet or the library to find out more about Pontius Pilate's governance of Palestine.

★ Study tip

It is important that you stick to the description of the trial before Pilate, as related by Mark. Do not include what you might have seen in films or read in other gospels.

Summary

You should now have knowledge of the trial of Jesus before Pilate. You should understand that Pilate agreed to the death penalty because the charge was treason and he thought it wise to do what the Sanhedrin was asking.

3.5 The crucifixion and burial of Jesus – Mark 15:21–47

> They compelled a passer-by, who was coming in from the country, to carry his cross; it was Simon of Cyrene, the father of Alexander and Rufus. Then they brought Jesus to the place called Golgotha (which means the place of a skull). And they offered him wine mixed with myrrh; but he did not take it. And they crucified him, and divided his clothes among them, casting lots to decide what each should take.
>
> It was nine o'clock in the morning when they crucified him. The inscription of the charge against him read, 'The King of the Jews.' And with him they crucified two bandits, one on his right and one on his left. Those who passed by derided him, shaking their heads and saying, 'Aha! You who would destroy the temple and build it in three days, save yourself, and come down from the cross!' In the same way the chief priests, along with the scribes, were also mocking him among themselves and saying, 'He saved others; he cannot save himself. Let the Messiah, the King of Israel, come down from the cross now, so that we may see and believe.' Those who were crucified with him also taunted him.
>
> When it was noon, darkness came over the whole land until three in the afternoon. At three o'clock Jesus cried out with a loud voice, 'Eloi, Eloi, lema sabachthani?' which means, 'My God, my God, why have you forsaken me?' When some of the bystanders heard it, they said, 'Listen, he is calling for Elijah.' And someone ran, filled a sponge with sour wine, put it on a stick, and gave it to him to drink, saying, 'Wait, let us see whether Elijah will come to take him down.' Then Jesus gave a loud cry and breathed his last. And the curtain of the temple was torn in two, from top to bottom. Now when the centurion, who stood facing him, saw that in this way he breathed his last, he said, 'Truly this man was God's son!'
>
> There were also women looking on from a distance, among them were Mary Magdalene, and Mary the mother of James the younger and of Joses, and Salome. These used to follow him and provided for him when he was in Galilee; and there were many other women who had come up with him to Jerusalem.
>
> When evening had come, and since it was the day of Preparation, that is, the day before the sabbath, Joseph of Arimathea, a respected member of the council, who was also himself waiting expectantly for the Kingdom of God, went boldly to Pilate and asked for the body of Jesus. Then Pilate wondered if he were already dead; and summoning the centurion, he asked him whether he had been dead for some time. When he learned from the centurion that he was dead, he granted the body to Joseph. Then Joseph bought a linen cloth, and taking down the body, wrapped it in the linen cloth, and laid it in a tomb that had been hewn out of the rock. He then rolled a stone against the door of the tomb. Mary Magdalene and Mary the mother of Joses saw where the body was laid.

Mark 15:21–47 [NRSV]

Objectives

- Study the crucifixion of Jesus and understand its importance and symbolism.
- Learn about the burial of Jesus and the beliefs around the importance of his death.

Key term

- **crucifixion:** 1. Roman method of execution by which criminals were fixed to a cross; 2. the execution and death of Jesus on Good Friday

⭐ Study tip

It is important that you learn the version of the crucifixion and burial as recorded by Mark. Write a list of the events that happened and the words used to help with your study.

Research activity

Look up Isaiah 53:12 and explain the connection with the crucifixion of Jesus.

Activities

1 Explain why the comment of the centurion is important.
2 Why was the burial of Jesus hurried?
3 Explain the importance of the women in the narrative.

■ The crucifixion

Crucifixion was a common punishment used by the Romans – particularly for those who had rebelled. The victim was left in agony to die. Many pictures show a sign attached to Jesus' cross which says 'INRI'. This is a short form of the Latin *'Iesus Nazarenus Rex Iudaeorum'* ('Jesus of Nazareth, King of the Jews'). Mark notes that wine mixed with myrrh was offered to Jesus as a painkiller, but he refused it.

There is no astronomical evidence of an eclipse at the time of Jesus' death. This could be a symbol of the removal of the Shekinah (the cosmic glory of God) light of God at that time. Mark states that the darkness was over the whole earth, showing that Jesus' death was to affect the whole world. Jesus' words in Aramaic 'Eloi, Eloi, lema sabachthani?' – 'My God, why have you forsaken me?' – are very important because they show that almost at the moment of death, Jesus felt separated from God. (The words are quoting psalm 22:1, a psalm of lament.)

According to Mark, although members of the crowd offered Jesus a drink, they thought that Elijah might come to save him. This is not surprising because it was Passover and the coming of Elijah was part of that Passover tradition. Also Jesus had used the word *'Eloi'* which may have been misheard as the name Elijah. The splitting of the curtain from top to bottom in the Temple is a symbol that through his death Jesus had removed sin, the barrier between God and humans.

■ The centurion's words

The centurion was an officer in the Roman army. His words, as a Gentile, are very significant. The statement of faith by the centurion, 'Truly this man was God's Son!' would have stood out as a comment from someone who was not Jewish, but nevertheless understood Jesus' divinity.

■ The meaning of Jesus' death for Christians today

Christians remember the death of Jesus on Good Friday. They believe that Jesus' death was important because:

- it was God's plan for the salvation of humanity
- Jesus fulfilled the Old Testament prophecies; he was the Messiah and the ultimate suffering servant
- Jesus shows a self-sacrificing love for all; he set an example to his followers that sometimes it is necessary to suffer or die for your beliefs
- Jesus' victory after suffering and dying, through the resurrection, would have been comforting and encouraging to many Christians reading the Gospel who were suffering from persecution.

Many Christians believe that the moment Jesus experienced a feeling of being deserted by God, he took on himself the sins of humanity and enabled people to get closer to God. They believe his death removed the barrier of sin and that Jesus restored the relationship with God so people are able to have their sins forgiven. Many Christians believe Jesus' crucifixion and resurrection shows that good is more powerful than evil and love stronger than hate.

▲ *A depiction of the crucifixion of Jesus by an unknown Spanish artist; it hangs in a church in Grenada*

Extension activity

Research the connection between the crucifixion and the forgiveness of sins.

Summary

You should now have an understanding of the events of the crucifixion and burial of Jesus and the reactions of those who were there.

> 66 When the sabbath was over, Mary Magdalene, and Mary the mother of James, and Salome bought spices, so that they might go and anoint him. And very early on the first day of the week, when the sun had risen, they went to the tomb. They had been saying to one another, 'Who will roll away the stone for us from the entrance to the tomb?' When they looked up, they saw that the stone, which was very large, had already been rolled back. As they entered the tomb, they saw a young man, dressed in a white robe, sitting on the right side; and they were alarmed. But he said to them, 'Do not be alarmed; you are looking for Jesus of Nazareth, who was crucified. He has been raised, he is not here. Look, there is the place they laid him. But go, tell his disciples and Peter that he is going ahead of you to Galilee; there you will see him, just as he told you.' So they went out and fled from the tomb, for terror and amazement had seized them; and they said nothing to anyone, for they were afraid. 99
>
> *Mark* 16:1–8 [NRSV]

Objective

● Learn about the resurrection narrative of Mark and examine some of the controversies around it.

Key term

● **resurrection:** 1. rising from the dead; 2. Jesus rising from the dead on Easter day; an event recorded in all four gospels and the central belief of Christianity

For most scholars, this passage is the end of Mark's Gospel. Many believe that the passage that follows in Mark 16:9–20 was added later to bring in the **resurrection** appearances and the commission.

■ The young man and the women

The women went to the tomb to anoint Jesus' body – to carry out the traditional Jewish burial customs that had not been followed because of the haste with which Jesus was buried. The young man is described by Mark as dressed in a white robe – the implication is that he was an angel. Angels were messengers of God. According to Mark, his message was that Jesus had risen from the dead, as he had told his disciples he would. He used the phrase 'do not be alarmed'. It is very likely that the women were alarmed because the main text of Mark ends with the words, 'They said nothing to anyone because they were afraid.'

▲ *The Garden Tomb in Jerusalem is a first-century tomb in a garden, very like the one in which Jesus was laid*

■ The empty tomb

The description of the empty tomb does not prove that Jesus rose from the dead, and theories emerged to discredit this claim. Quite soon after this incident, the disciples began to preach that Jesus had risen from the dead (Acts 2). Christians argue that there is evidence for the authority of the account and for the fact that Jesus rose from the dead:

• The women witnessed the empty tomb.

• There were later sightings of Jesus recorded in the New Testament.

Extension activity

Research views about the different endings to Mark's Gospel. Did Mark originally end his account with a reference to the women being afraid? If so, suggest reasons why he might have done so.

- The exact location of the tomb was forgotten – it was unimportant as Jesus was believed to have risen from the dead.
- Christians were tortured and killed for their faith. Would they have accepted this for something they did not believe to be true?
- The resurrection completes Jesus' teaching and proves that he was the Son of God.
- The resurrection proves God's plan that Jesus had cemented a new relationship with God.

The arguments against the idea that Jesus rose from the dead and their counterarguments may be summed up as follows:

Arguments that Jesus did not rise	Counterarguments
The disciples took the body.	Is it likely that a group of men, who were so frightened by what had happened to Jesus, would steal a body and try to conceal it?
The Jewish authorities may have taken the body to stop any claims about resurrection.	Why did they not produce the body later? Also the Jews believed that to touch a dead body would have made them unclean.
The Romans took the body.	The Romans thought Jesus was just another irritating teacher from Galilee and leader of an insignificant group of Galileans.
The women went to the wrong place.	Mark explains that they watched carefully where Jesus was laid.
They were all hallucinating.	This may have been what the disciples first thought, but there is little evidence for mass hallucinations.
Jesus did not really die and merely recovered in the cool of the tomb.	A Roman centurion would have known when a man was dead.
It was a ghost.	In other gospels Jesus is shown to have eaten after the resurrection. He is recognised as a person.

■ Beliefs about the resurrection today

The belief that Jesus rose from the dead is essential to the Christian faith because it shows Christians that good is more powerful than evil, and that suffering cannot separate people from the love of God. The resurrection demonstrates God's power, and Christians believe it proves that Jesus' teaching can be relied upon. Christians believe that Christ is alive and present with them.

Belief in the resurrection means that Christians believe in the hope of life after death and life with God, so death is not something to fear. Some Christians believe that everyone will rise from the dead and one day Jesus will return (this is known as the Parousia). When he does, the Kingdom of God – a kingdom of justice, mercy and peace – will be established.

The resurrection is commemorated by Christians every year on Easter Day, and there are many rituals associated with it around the world. Easter is the most important festival for Christians.

> **Discussion activity**
>
> Discuss in a group whether you think it matters if the resurrection happened or not.

> **Activities**
>
> 1 How do you think the women would have felt after seeing the empty tomb?
>
> 2 Could belief in the resurrection be proved to be wrong? If it were, what would that mean for Christianity?

> ★ **Study tip**
>
> You must learn the details of the resurrection account as it is recorded in Mark's Gospel and not confuse it with the other gospel narratives.

> **Summary**
>
> You should now have considered some of the debate about the empty tomb and understand the importance of the resurrection of Jesus for Christians.

> **Activity**
>
> 'The resurrection is the most important event in Mark's Gospel. Nothing else matters.' Do you agree? Give reasons for your answer.

The early ministry of Jesus – summary

You should now be able to:

✔ explain differing views on the authority of St Mark's Gospel

✔ demonstrate knowledge about the work of John the Baptist and his importance in understanding the ministry of Jesus

✔ explain the importance of baptism in the first century and today

✔ explain the meanings of the different titles of Jesus used in St Mark's Gospel

✔ demonstrate knowledge of the text of the baptism and temptation of Jesus, and explain what it meant to him and to others

✔ demonstrate knowledge of the text of the healing of the paralysed man and Jairus' daughter, and explain the role of faith in healing and the authority of Jesus

✔ explain why Jesus was rejected in Nazareth

✔ demonstrate knowledge of the text of the feeding of the 5000 and explain its importance in understanding Jesus as the Messiah

✔ consider debates about the miracles of Jesus.

The later ministry of Jesus – summary

You should now be able to:

✔ demonstrate knowledge about the conversation between Jesus and the disciples at Caesarea Philippi and understand its importance

✔ explain the concept of the Messianic Secret in St Mark's Gospel

✔ demonstrate knowledge about the transfiguration of Jesus and explain its importance to the disciples and believers

✔ explain Jesus' passion prediction

✔ explain what the question from James and John about their place in heaven and Jesus' answer teaches believers

✔ explain what is understood about messianic expectation in the first century CE

✔ describe and explain the importance of the healing of Bartimaeus

✔ describe and explain the meaning of the entry of Jesus into Jerusalem

✔ explain the importance of faith in St Mark's Gospel and today.

The final days in Jerusalem – summary

You should now be able to:

✔ describe the events of the Last Supper, explain the meanings of the words and actions of Jesus

✔ describe the events in Gethsemane and explain what the incident means for the understanding of the role of Jesus

✔ explain what happened at the trial of Jesus before the Jewish authorities, and what happened at the trial before Pilate

✔ describe events at the crucifixion of Jesus as recorded in St Mark's Gospel, the meaning of it for the early Church and Christians today

✔ explain what happened at the burial of Jesus and beliefs about the importance of his death

✔ explain Mark's account of the empty tomb and different explanations given for what happened.

Sample student answer – the 4-mark question

1. Write an answer to the following question:

    Explain two contrasting ways in which Christians believe that Mark's Gospel is relevant today. **[4 marks]**

2. Read the following student sample answer:

    "Mark's Gospel is still relevant today because the problems that people faced in the past are still there. People are still ill and they are looking for healing. In the story of the healing of Jairus' daughter the father asked Jesus to come to save his daughter. That is just like people praying today. The other reasons it is relevant is that people believe that Jesus is the Son of God and it helps them to see what that means for them, especially in the resurrection of Jesus, which gives them a certainty of life after death."

3. With a partner discuss the sample answer. Is the focus of the answer correct? Is anything missing from the answer? How do you think it could be improved?

4. What mark (out of 4) would you give this answer? Look at the mark scheme in the Introduction (AO1). What are the reasons for the mark you have given?

5. Now swap your answer with your partner's and mark each other's responses. What mark (out of 4) would you give the response? Refer to the mark scheme and give reasons for the mark you award.

Sample student answer – the 5-mark question

1. Write and answer to the following question:

    Explain two reasons why Christians believe that Jesus' death was necessary.

    You must refer to St Mark's Gospel in your answer. **[5 marks]**

2. Read the following student sample answer:

    Christians believe that Jesus' death was necessary because Jesus predicted it himself. At Caesarea Philippi Jesus predicted that he would die and rise again. Without Jesus' death the resurrection would not have been possible. This is the basis for the Christian faith.

    Another reason that Christians give is that Jesus had to die on behalf of everyone. In Jewish tradition there was a need for a blood sacrifice to be given to God in the Temple. Jesus sacrificed himself for humanity when he was crucified at Jerusalem. Christians have referred to this as the atonement. Sins were forgiven because Jesus died.

3. With a partner discuss the sample answer. Is the focus of the answer correct? Is nything missing from the answer? How do you think it could be improved?

4. What mark (out of 5) would you give this answer? Look at the mark scheme in the Introduction (AO1). What are the reasons for the mark you have given?

5. Now swap your answer with your partner's and mark each other's responses. What mark (out of 5) would you give the response? Refer to the mark scheme and give reasons for the mark you award.

Sample student answer – the 12-mark question

1. Write an answer to the following question:

'The baptism of Jesus was more important than the transfiguration.'

Evaluate this statement. In your answer you:
- should give reasoned arguments to support this statement
- should give reasoned arguments to support a different point of view
- should refer to St Mark's Gospel
- may refer to non-religious arguments
- should reach a justified conclusion.

[12 marks]
[+ 3 SPaG marks]

2. Read the following student sample answer:

Both the baptism and the transfiguration are important. I will explain which is the most important and why.

The baptism was the beginning of Jesus' ministry. He was to stop being a carpenter and go out preaching and healing. After the baptism, when Jesus was praying, Mark says the Holy Spirit appeared in the form of a dove, and there was a voice from heaven which said, 'You are my son, with you I am well pleased.' This voice was God's.

The voice from God was really important because it looks as if everyone heard it and the dove means that the Trinity were there (God the Father, Son and Holy Spirit). It set an example for all Christians later that baptism was something that should happen. It is a sign of God being with you and your new life beginning. Many believe that sins are washed away.

The transfiguration was after Peter had said that Jesus was the Christ. Jesus, Peter, James and John went up a mountain and there Jesus became shining white in front of them. Moses and Elijah appeared and seemed to be talking to Jesus. Then there was a cloud and a voice from heaven again said, 'This is my son, listen to him.'

This showed Jesus as a glorious person. He was pulling together the Law (Moses) and the Prophets (Elijah), and following his religion. It was only witnessed by three disciples. It would have been more important to later believers if there were more witnesses. Some people who don't believe in Christianity might think that this is made up.

I think that the baptism is the most important because it is still done today to babies and adults.

3. With a partner discuss the student sample answer. Consider the following questions:
- Does the answer focus on the questions asked?
- Does the answer refer to Mark's Gospel, and if so what are they?
- Is there an argument to support the statement and how well developed is it?
- Is there a different point of view offered and how well developed is that argument?
- Has the student written a clear conclusion after weighing up both sides of the argument?
- Are there logical steps in the argument?
- What is good about this answer?
- How do you think it could be improved?

4. What mark (out of 12) would you give this answer? Look at the mark scheme in the introduction (AO2). What are the reasons for the mark you have given?

5. Now swap your answer to the question with your partner's and mark each other's responses. What mark (out of 12) would you give their answer? Refer to the mark scheme and give reasons for the mark you award.

Practice questions

1 What was the name of the blind man whom Jesus healed in Jericho?

A) Jairus   **B)** Bartimaeus   **C)** Judas   **D)** Barnabas   **[1 mark]**

2 Give **two** ways, recorded by St Mark, in which Jesus demonstrated that he was the Messiah.   **[2 marks]**

 Study tip

This question can be answered with just a phrase or a sentence. The 'ways' do not need development.

3 Explain **two** reasons ways why Jesus chose to call himself Son of Man rather than Son of God during his ministry.   **[4 marks]**

 Study tip

You should show that you know what the titles Son of Man and Son of God mean and then explain why Jesus called himself Son of Man.

4 Give **two** reasons why Jesus was rejected by many during his ministry.
You must refer to St Mark's Gospel in your answer.   **[5 marks]**

 Study tip

Before writing your answer think carefully about the reasons you could use to explain this. Try to remember to include a reference to Mark's Gospel in your answer.

5 'Jesus only helped those with faith.'

Evaluate this statement. In your answer you:

- should give reasoned arguments to support this statement
- should give reasoned arguments to support a different point of view
- should refer to St Mark's Gospel
- may refer to non-religious arguments
- should reach a justified conclusion.

     [12 marks]
     [+ 3 SPaG marks]

 **Study tip**

Read the statement carefully and check that you have followed the bullet points in the question. You should aim to refer to at least two incidents in your answer (more if you have time) and make it clear what Jesus did to help and whether the people demonstrated faith. Choose important parts to refer to in your answer. You can offer your own views on whether faith matters in asking for help, for example when praying.

Part 2: Mark's Gospel as a source of religious, moral and spiritual truths

4 The Kingdom of God

4.1 The Parable of the Sower – Mark 4:1–9, 14–20

> " Again he began to teach beside the lake. Such a very large crowd gathered around him that he got into a boat on the lake and sat there; while the whole crowd was beside the lake on the land. He began to teach them many things in parables, and in his teaching he said to them: 'Listen! A sower went out to sow. And as he sowed, some seed fell on the path, and the birds came and ate it up. Other seed fell on rocky ground, where it did not have much soil, and it sprang up quickly, since it had no depth of soil. And when the sun rose, it was scorched; and since it had no root, it withered away. Other seed fell among thorns, and the thorns grew up and choked it, and it yielded no grain. Other seed fell into good soil and brought forth grain, growing up and increasing and yielding thirty and sixty and a hundredfold.' And he said, 'Let anyone with ears to hear listen!' …
>
> The sower sows the word. These are the ones on the path where the word is sown: when they hear, Satan immediately comes and takes away the word which is sown in them. And these are the ones sown on rocky ground: when they hear the word, they immediately receive it with joy. But they have no root, and endure only for a while; then, when trouble or persecution arises on account of the word, immediately they fall away. And others are those sown among the thorns: these are the ones who hear the word, but the cares of the world, and the lure of wealth, and the desire for other things come in and choke the word, and it yields nothing. And these are the ones sown on the good soil: they hear the word and accept it and bear fruit, thirty and sixty and a hundredfold. "
>
> *Mark 4:1–9, 14–20* [NRSV]

The Kingdom of God is an essential part of Jesus' teaching in Mark's Gospel. Mark describes how Jesus created a vision of how life should be lived on earth, but also described life with God beyond death, a life where God ruled eternally.

Jesus told **parables** to challenge and educate his listeners. They were short stories but they would all leave the hearer with a message or something to think about. They can be interpreted in different ways and often have been adapted to meet different times and social situations.

Objective

- Understand the idea of the Kingdom of God and be able to understand its connection with the Parable of the Sower.

Key terms

- **parable:** a story with spiritual meaning told by Jesus to challenge listeners and teach them about their relationship with God
- **allegory:** a story where the spiritual message is given using non-spiritual images, each of which can easily be replaced to show the true meaning

Activities

1 Make a list of the things that could distract people from faith today.

2 Do people hear the message of Jesus today? Explain your answer.

3 'If Jesus were alive today he would have a website.' What do you think? Give reasons for your answer.

■ An agricultural community

It is not surprising that a number of Jesus' parables are linked to agricultural images such as seeds, the harvest and reaping. Jesus and his followers knew the farming methods of the day. They would have seen the workers sowing seeds by hand and scattering them in all directions. They would also have known the importance of the harvest that followed. These images would have been very clear to Jesus' audience. Some people might use this as an argument to say that the stories do not apply to the present day and are out of date. The key element of a parable, though, is not the story itself but the message that is being delivered.

▲ The image of someone sowing seeds would have been well known to Jesus' audience

■ Understanding the parable

According to Mark, the disciples did not understand. Others who heard probably did not understand either. Jesus then offered them the explanation. In doing so, he emphasised the importance of faithful discipleship, and the need to share his message with others. The disciples might not have realised at the time how important this would become for them later.

In this parable, Jesus used the form of an **allegory** to teach the disciples. In an allegory the individual elements of a story stand for something else in particular. Not all parables are allegories and it is not appropriate to try to make them all allegories.

Parable	Explanation
Farmer	The preacher or teacher
Seed	The word of God, the message
Birds	Satan, the devil
Seed on the path	People who hear the news but who are not committed enough to do anything about it – it is taken from them.
Seed in the rocks	People who are delighted to hear the news, but their faith is not deeply rooted in them so when trouble or persecution comes, they give up.
Seed in the thorns	People who are too interested in worldly goods and pleasures to become true disciples. They hear the message but do nothing.
Seed on the good soil	People who hear the message and accept it; they become disciples and share the news with others so the Kingdom grows.

The emphasis in this parable is that disciples must hear. The Kingdom can grow only if the message is heard. However, the Kingdom grows abundantly once it is heard and acted upon. The parable would also encourage the early Christians to stick to their faith in the face of difficulties. Modern believers can face the same difficulties and distractions from faith, so can feel encouraged by this parable to persevere. In doing so they believe they will see the Kingdom of God grow.

Research activity 🔍

There are a number of Christian radio stations around the world, such as the Vatican Radio http://en.radiovaticana.va/ and Premier Radio http://www.premier.org.uk/. There are also numerous Christian and other religious broadcasters on satellite television. Discuss with your group whether you think these are a good way of spreading the message.

⭐ Study tip

Learn carefully the four types of ground, and the four reactions of people to the message they are receiving.

Summary

You should now understand the meaning of the Parable of the Sower and be able see how it relates to the growth of the Kingdom of God.

The Parable of the Growing Seed – Mark 4:26–29

> " He also said, 'The Kingdom of God is as if someone would scatter seed on the ground, and would sleep and rise night and day, and the seed would sprout and grow, he does not know how. The earth produces of itself, first the stalk, then the head, then the full grain in the head. But when the grain is ripe, at once he goes in with his sickle, because the harvest has come.' "
>
> *Mark 4:26–29* [NRSV]

Objective

- Study the Parable of the Growing Seed and understand its meaning.

According to Jesus' teaching a key feature of the Kingdom of God is that it would grow greatly, and that people would be taken by surprise at the rate that it grew. The sower in this parable did not understand how the seed grew, but he knew it did, because harvest time arrived. At the beginning of his gospel, Mark includes Jesus' teaching that 'the Kingdom of God has come near' (Mark 1:15). Jesus wanted the Kingdom to begin to grow in his lifetime and continue after the resurrection. It was part of the disciples' responsibility to ensure that this would happen. Jesus' listeners would easily understand the use of seeds as an image of growth.

▲ *The seeds from which wheat grows*

■ The growing seed

This parable is found only in Mark's Gospel. Like the Parable of the Sower, the image is of a man scattering seeds. It is a very simple story that describes how the seed grows whatever the man does. This may have been a warning to the Zealots, who thought that the Kingdom of God could be brought in through violence. In this sense, Jesus was illustrating the idea that the Kingdom grows whatever those who are working to bring it in do. The Kingdom has a life of its own. The description of the three stages reflects the growth and then comes the harvest. The sower has waited faithfully for the seed to grow and his patience has been rewarded.

In the Old Testament the harvest is a metaphor for judgement (e.g. Joel 3:13). Throughout Jesus' teaching there is the idea that the harvest will come, and this will be where all will be judged. Jesus had confidence that this would take place. This parable is not the beginning of a debate between Jesus and his hearers; it is clearly a teaching for the disciples (and all Christians) that they should have a similar faith in the steady growth of the Kingdom that will come, as long as they keep their confidence in God.

▲ *This parable teaches Christians that the Kingdom of God will grow like wheat in a field*

⭐ **Study tip**

Make sure that you are clear about the different parables which involve seeds – do not confuse them.

■ Understanding this parable today

In many parts of the world the Christian Church is being persecuted. In some places (such as Western Europe) there is a decline in traditional church attendance. Christians can become disheartened and begin to believe that the Kingdom is not growing at all. But in this parable it is clear that the Kingdom will grow because it is God's will that it does. This can be a source of encouragement for persecuted Christians and those feeling that there is no future for the Church. This parable may reassure believers that the future may be different (as a seed transforms into a bush) so they should keep their faith and be patient.

Parables of the Kingdom of God are not about a great shining and powerful kingdom with great splendour. They show a kingdom that will come quietly and slowly but certainly.

The Jewish people in the first century CE knew from their history that earthly kingdoms come and go. The same is true in the modern world. After the Second World War, a large Soviet empire existed that was hostile to Christianity. Under the empire's rule, there were some authorised religious activities which were carefully controlled, but there were others which had to become underground movements. Believers ran great risks by meeting secretly. The Soviet Empire has now gone and Christianity has an opportunity to develop. The number of practising Christians may be growing in these countries but it is difficult to say for sure how much the Kingdom of God is growing there, because it is a spiritual Kingdom.

The growth of Christianity in China

China is on track to become the nation with the highest Christian population by 2030. Professor Yang, a leading expert on religion in China, believes that the number of Christians in China will grow to about 160 million by 2025. That would likely mean that there will be more Christians in China than in the United States. The 5000-capacity Liushi Church has more than twice as many seats as Westminster Abbey in London, and a crucifix more than 60m high that can be seen for miles around.

▲ *The enormous Liushi Church was built in a comparatively small town in China*

Activities

1 Explain, in your own words, the meaning of the parable.

2 Why would this parable be encouraging for the early Christian Church?

3 Do you think that the idea of a growing seed to describe the growth of the Kingdom of God is a helpful image? Explain your answer.

Discussion activity

Discuss with your group whether it is likely that the Kingdom of God will ever come on earth.

Extension activity

Some people think that this parable helps Christians to learn about life after death. What do you think? Explain the reasons for your view.

Summary

You should now know the Parable of the Growing Seed and understand its meaning.

The Parable of the Mustard Seed – Mark 4:30–32

> **"** He also said, 'With what can we compare the Kingdom of God, or what parable shall we use for it? It is like a mustard seed, which, when sown upon the ground, is the smallest of all the seeds on earth; yet when it is sown it grows up and becomes the greatest of all shrubs, and puts forth large branches, so that the birds of the air can make nests in its shade.' **"**
>
> *Mark* 4:30–32 [NRSV]

Objective

- Study the Parable of the Mustard Seed and understand what it teaches about the Kingdom of God.

▲ *Mustard seeds are among the smallest seeds in Palestine*

■ Understanding this parable

The strength of Jesus' parables come from the fact that they all used images that people at the time could imagine easily. In this short parable the minute size of a mustard seed is compared with the bush or tree that can grow from it. The people who heard this would be very familiar with the mustard seed and its bush. The seed is not actually the smallest in Palestine but it is very small. The bush that grows from it is large enough for birds to nest in. This growth is not a result of human effort. It is a gift from God through the working of nature. Jesus was teaching his followers that the Kingdom starts out hidden, small and insignificant, but then it grows (unseen at first) and becomes a substantial size.

There is a link between this parable and the entry of Jesus into Jerusalem. Jesus entered not as a king, but in a very peaceful way, riding not on a horse but on a donkey – yet he was still recognised as the Messiah. This is another example of an apparently small act resulting eventually in something large enough to change the world.

The reference to the birds nesting in the branches is an indication that the Kingdom of God is for all – Jews and Gentiles. In the Old Testament there are a number of references to the Gentiles being included in God's chosen people. One example is Psalm 104:12: 'By the streams the birds of the air have their habitation; they sing among the branches.' The parable can also be related to the book of Daniel:

▲ *The crop that grows from the tiny mustard seed is very large*

> **"** Upon my bed this is what I saw; there was a tree at the centre of the earth, and its height was great. The tree grew great and strong, its top reached to heaven, and it was visible to the ends of the whole earth. Its foliage was beautiful, and its fruit abundant, and it provided food for all. The animals of the field found shade under it, the birds of the air nested in its branches, and from it all living beings were fed. **"**
>
> *Daniel* 4:10–12 [NRSV]

Links

See pages 34–35 to read about Jesus' entry into Jerusalem.

■ Understanding the Kingdom of God

Jesus' teaching on the Kingdom of God occurs throughout Mark's Gospel. It is not a place, but describes the influence of God, God's rule. Jesus taught:

- that the Kingdom is a present reality (already here on earth) – in Mark 1:15 Jesus told his hearers, 'The Kingdom of God has come near; repent, and believe in the good news.'

- that the Kingdom will also come in the future(at some point all would do God's will) – in Mark 9:1, Jesus taught that some of the people standing listening to him 'will not taste death until they see that the Kingdom of God has come with power.'

- about the Kingdom's characteristics, such as its fast growth

- that wealth may be a barrier to entry to the Kingdom; it must be used wisely

- that it is about keeping the commandments, not just the 613 rules of the Jewish Law, but the two commandments that Jesus said were the most important: love God and love your neighbour

- that having the innocence of a child will enable people to enter the Kingdom of God

- that discipleship is essential to the Kingdom

- that the Kingdom of God is about hope – Joseph of Arimathea is described by Mark as 'waiting expectantly for the Kingdom of God' (Mark 15:43)

- that it is not a political Kingdom, although the Zealots hoped that it would be – Jesus taught a gospel of peace

- that his miracles were signs of the Kingdom.

■ The Kingdom of God today

In the Lord's Prayer, Christians pray, 'your Kingdom come, your will be done, on earth as it is in heaven'. In saying this, Christians are praying that the Kingdom of God will be established on earth now. This motivates many Christians to volunteer to work in their community and to join a worshipping community, or to work full time serving their community. Some take religious orders and vows. Many churches run food banks to try to ensure that the poorest have enough to eat, or provide other activities to show that people are valued and cared for – all characteristics of the Kingdom of God.

Many Christian organisations, like the World Council of Churches, Christian Aid, CAFOD and Tearfund, work to show people across the world that they are cared for and that they are God's people. Christians also become involved in the work of organisations like the United Nations, especially where there are opportunities to volunteer, and where people of many races and religions can make a difference to the quality of people's lives.

Activities

1 The image of the birds sitting in the shade in the branches of the tree suggests a safe place. How would a persecuted Christian understand this message?

2 'The parables of Jesus have great meaning for Christians today.' Evaluate this statement, showing that you have thought about more than one point of view.

3 Explain ways in which Christians believe they can work for the Kingdom of God.

4 Should Christians involve themselves in politics to bring about the Kingdom of God? Explain the reasons for your answer.

Links

See pages 60–61 for details on the teaching that wealth will be a barrier to entry to the Kingdom of God.

There is more about childhood innocence enabling people to enter the Kingdom on pages 58–59.

⭐ Study tip

Remember that Christians believe that the Kingdom of God is growing at all times.

Summary

You have now read and studied three parables about the growth of the Kingdom of God and should understand what they teach about the Kingdom.

4.4 Jesus and the children – Mark 10:13–16

> ❝ People were bringing little children to him in order that he might touch them; and the disciples spoke sternly to them. But when Jesus saw this, he was indignant and said to them, 'Let the little children come to me; do not stop them; for it is to such as these that the Kingdom of God belongs. Truly I tell you, whoever does not receive the Kingdom of God as a little child will never enter it.' And he took them up in his arms, laid his hands on them, and blessed them. ❞
>
> *Mark* 10:13–16 [NRSV]

Objective

- Study Jesus' meeting with the children and understand what he teaches about the Kingdom of God.

Childhood in Palestine in the first century CE was very different from today. Children were sent to work at young ages (possibly five or six years old) and many were married and had begun their family by their mid-teens. A boy was regarded as an adult after his bar mitzvah ceremony, usually at the age of 13. After this he was considered an adult, and able to accept responsibilities. A working man could normally only expect to live between 35 and 40 years. It is likely that the children brought to Jesus would have been very young indeed. They may even have been babies in arms. This passage is placed by Mark just after Jesus had been teaching about marriage and divorce, so fits very well.

▲ Some depictions of this event, such as this from Lucas Cranach the Elder, show the children to be babies, whereas in others they are older

■ 'Laid his hands on them'

Touch is a very powerful thing. Jesus very often touched those he was going to cure. However, in this account the touch that the parents were looking for was one that gave a blessing to their child. Jewish people believed that touch could give a blessing. In some cases, touch was used to show which son was to inherit everything. The rabbis of the first century used to have children sent to them for a blessing. In Genesis 27 there is the account of Isaac blessing Jacob and Esau. Touch was so important that Jacob had to put on goatskins so that the blind Isaac would not recognise him when he touched him.

Notice that Jesus was apparently unhappy with his disciples' reactions. According to Mark, the disciples did not behave well at this event, although it is likely they were trying to protect Jesus. Mark reports that Jesus did not appreciate their efforts. The word 'rebuked' is also used to describe when Jesus exorcised demons (e.g. Mark 1:25, when Jesus commanded the unclean spirit to come out of the possessed man).

■ Jesus' words and actions

Jesus recognised that these children were powerless and helpless. According to Mark, he wanted them to come to him. By taking them in his arms (one translation is that he 'hugged them'), he was able to explain a teaching about the Kingdom of God, as well as reassure the parents. Mark writes that Jesus told the disciples that the only way people could enter the Kingdom of God was to be like a child. Childlike characteristics may include innocence, humility and lack of selfishness. Jesus was teaching that if people approach the Kingdom of God like a child, they will be accepted, and that if someone believes, they will accept God's teachings and way of life.

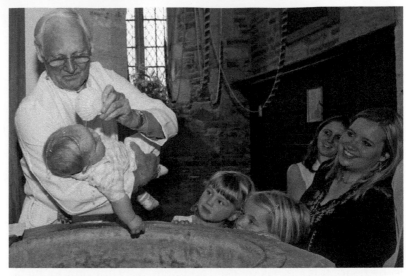

▲ *Some Christian communities believe this account supports the practice of baptising babies or young children*

■ Infant baptism

This passage has influenced churches which practise infant baptism, even though Jesus did not here baptise the children, he only blessed them. These Christians say that if Jesus brought children into the Kingdom by blessing them, then babies may join the Church through baptism. This is particularly true in Catholic, Anglican, and some non-conformist traditions. For example, this passage from Mark was printed in the 1662 Book of Common Prayer to be read in a service of baptism, and some Church of England, as well as other churches, use it when conducting an infant baptism. Other traditions do not practise infant baptism and in the Baptist tradition, for example, a child is dedicated and blessed, but must wait until they can make their own decision to be baptised.

Many Christians today think it is important to welcome children into congregations because they are the future of the Christian Church. Parents are encouraged to bring children to church, and in many places there are special services for them. If Jesus had not welcomed children, then people might think the Church is only for adults. Jesus set an example by including everyone in his teaching.

> ❝ The practice of infant baptism is an immemorial tradition of the Church. There is explicit testimony to this practice from the second century on, and it is quite possible that, from the beginning of the apostolic preaching, when whole 'households' received baptism, infants may also have been baptised. ❞
>
> *Catechism of the Catholic Church,* paragraph 1252

Activities

1 Discuss with your group whether you think this passage from Mark's Gospel supports infant baptism.

2 Was faith being demonstrated in this incident? If so, who was showing faith?

3 'If the disciples had succeeded in preventing the children from coming to Jesus, Christianity would have been different.' What do you think? Give reasons for your answer.

⭐ Study tip

Remember that Jesus demonstrated in this incident that the Kingdom of God was for all ages.

Summary

You should now know about Jesus blessing the children and how this has affected the tradition of baptism in the Christian Church.

> **"** As he was setting out on a journey, a man ran up and knelt before him, and asked him, 'Good Teacher, what must I do to inherit eternal life?' Jesus said to him, 'Why do you call me good? No one is good but God alone. You know the commandments: "You shall not murder; You shall not commit adultery; You shall not steal; You shall not bear false witness; You shall not defraud; Honour your father and mother."' He said to him, 'Teacher, I have kept all these since my youth.' Jesus, looking at him, loved him and said, 'You lack one thing; go, sell what you own, and give the money to the poor, and you will have treasure in heaven; then come, follow me.' When he heard this, he was shocked and went away grieving, for he had many possessions.
>
> Then Jesus looked around and said to his disciples, 'How hard it will be for those who have wealth to enter the Kingdom of God!' And the disciples were perplexed at these words. But Jesus said to them again, 'Children, how hard it is to enter the Kingdom of God! It is easier for a camel to go through the eye of a needle than for someone who is rich to enter the Kingdom of God.' They were greatly astounded and said to one another, 'Then who can be saved?' Jesus looked at them and said, 'For mortals it is impossible, but not for God; for God all things are possible.' **"**
>
> *Mark* 10:17–27 [NRSV]

■ The rich man's question

The rich man from this passage was clearly one of the Jews who believed in life after death. The concept of eternal life, or a life after death, was not universally accepted in Jewish society. The Pharisees believed it, but the Sadducees did not. According to Mark, the rich man understood that his actions could affect his chance to gain eternal life, but he did not know what he should do. It is not clear how much of Jesus' teaching the man had heard, but it was certainly enough to convince him that Jesus could guide him to act in such a way that would be rewarded after death.

Mark writes that the man asked him how to live a good life, and not how to be a disciple. In the first century CE Jews believed that the way you lived was important. The teaching was known as *halakah*. This means literally 'to walk' and refers to the belief that people should 'walk' in the way of the Law and the rabbis' teaching. This man felt that he was living a good life. People at the time believed that riches were a reward from God for good living.

The man called Jesus 'good'. Jesus responded that no one is good but God. It is possible that Jesus here was indicating to the man that if he thought Jesus was good he might believe that he was God, or perhaps he was pointing the man to God, rather than himself – possibly both. It may be an example of the Messianic Secret. Jesus did not want the man to be casual in his use of the word 'good'.

Objectives

- Study the question of the rich man and Jesus' answers.
- Understand what Jesus' teaching might mean for Christian disciples.

▲ *Jesus again used an image which would be familiar to his listeners to explain his teaching – the image of a camel*

Activities

1 What answer do you think the rich man expected when he asked Jesus his question?

2 'It is hard to pray when your fridge is full.' Do you agree? Give reasons for your answer.

3 Explain why some Christians believe this advice was given to one particular man, and was not an instruction to all his followers.

Research activity

Use a website like www.biblegateway.com to look at how Mark uses the word 'amazed' in his gospel. Note who is amazed and why.

■ Jesus' answer

According to Mark, Jesus answered the man by reciting five of the Ten Commandments. He added also 'You shall not defraud', which reflected his interest in those who were in need. Almost any rabbi of the time could have given that answer. The man perhaps expected more because he replied, in effect, 'Yes, but I have already done that.'

Jesus did not comment on the man's self-certainty but showed him love. By using the word 'love', Mark means that Jesus was seeking the man's wellbeing. Although the man was sure he had done the right things, his question showed Jesus that he had the right childlike qualities to bring him into the Kingdom of God.

Jesus then told the rich man to sell everything and give the proceeds to the poor and 'follow me'. Jesus had used those words when he called the first disciples (Mark 1:17). They were not required to give everything away, but had to leave it behind. This was part of the cost of discipleship. Jesus' response was not what the man would have expected. He could not do this and went away sadly. He fits well into the category of the seeds who fell among the weeds in the Parable of the Sower – he is choked by worldly possessions.

> **Links**
>
> See pages 52–53 to read the Parable of the Sower.

■ The Kingdom of God

Jesus used this brief incident to teach the disciples something else about the Kingdom. Riches can act as a barrier to entering the Kingdom of God. Once again the disciples were amazed. Nevertheless, Mark shows how Jesus was very clear in his teaching. He called them children – perhaps a reference to his teaching about children – and then used the odd phrase 'it is easier for a camel to go through the eye of a needle than for someone who is rich to enter the Kingdom of God'. In the past Bible experts believed that the 'eye of the needle' might refer to a small gate in the city wall. However, there is no evidence at all of such a gate existing in Jerusalem until the ninth century CE. It is quite likely that Jesus simply used an impossible image in order to make the point that riches are a barrier to entry into the Kingdom of God.

▲ *Nuns are expected to give away their possessions before they can take their vows*

Finally Jesus made it very clear to the disciples that everything is in God's hands. People cannot earn or buy their place in heaven.

> ⭐ **Study tip**
>
> Do not confuse this incident with the man who asked Jesus what the most important commandment was (pages 62–63).

■ Christians and riches

Christians believe that Jesus was teaching that this man's wealth presented a barrier against his approach to God. It prevented him from seeing the priorities, from being sufficiently sensitive, perhaps, to people's needs. Christians do not believe that wealth is a reward for goodness. They believe that privilege of wealth brings responsibility, and people who have been given their riches by God need to use them for the good of all.

> **Summary**
>
> You should now know about an incident in which Jesus demonstrated that riches can be a barrier to discipleship and the Kingdom of God.

> One of the scribes came near and heard them disputing with one another, and seeing that he answered them well, he asked him, 'Which commandment is the first of all?' Jesus answered, 'The first is, "Hear, O Israel: the Lord our God, the Lord is one; and you shall love the Lord your God with all your heart, and with all your soul, and with all your mind, and with all your strength." The second is this, "You shall love your neighbour as yourself." There is no other commandment greater than these.' Then the scribe said to him, 'You are right, Teacher; you have truly said that "he is one, and besides him there is no other"; and "to love him with all the heart, and with all the understanding, and with all the strength", and "to love one's neighbour as oneself",—this is much more important than all whole burnt-offerings and sacrifices.' When Jesus saw that he answered wisely, he said to him, 'You are not far from the Kingdom of God.' After that no one dared to ask him any question.
>
> *Mark 12:28–34 [NRSV]*

Objectives

- Learn which of the commandments that Jesus taught were the most important.
- Understand reasons for this teaching.

Key term

- **Shema:** the Jewish statement of faith

■ The question

The question asked by a teacher of the Law in this passage is one of four questions put to Jesus in Mark 12. Mark writes that Jesus entered Jerusalem and was then tested by a series of questions. Some of them may have been designed to catch him out, but this question about the greatest commandment was probably not one of these. We know from Jewish writings that many rabbis were asked this question.

It is quite likely that the man did not get the answer he was expecting. The Jews had many commandments (613 in all), but he was probably asking which of the Ten Commandments was the most important. Those listening would have been interested to see if Jesus could be accused of blasphemy. If he did not say the first commandment, 'I am the Lord your God … you shall have no other gods before me' (Deuteronomy 5:6–7), he might have been accused of blasphemy for not putting God first.

■ Jesus' answer

Jesus answered with two verses taken from different parts of the Old Testament. The first is part of the **Shema**, the Jewish statement of faith found in Deuteronomy 6:4: 'Hear, O Israel: The Lord is our God, the Lord alone. You shall love the Lord your God with all your heart, and with all your soul, and with all your might.' Jesus added to this that one should love God with all one's mind. This statement was thought to sum up the whole of the

שְׁמַע יִשְׂרָאֵל יְיָ אֱלֹהֵינוּ, יְיָ | אֶחָד:

בָּרוּךְ שֵׁם כְּבוֹד מַלְכוּתוֹ לְעוֹלָם וָעֶד:

וְאָהַבְתָּ אֵת יְיָ אֱלֹהֶיךָ, בְּכָל־לְבָבְךָ, וּבְכָל־נַפְשְׁךָ, וּבְכָל־מְאֹדֶךָ: וְהָיוּ הַדְּבָרִים הָאֵלֶּה, אֲשֶׁר אָנֹכִי מְצַוְּךָ הַיּוֹם, עַל לְבָבֶךָ: וְשִׁנַּנְתָּם לְבָנֶיךָ וְדִבַּרְתָּ בָּם, בְּשִׁבְתְּךָ בְּבֵיתֶךָ וּבְלֶכְתְּךָ בַדֶּרֶךְ וּבְשָׁכְבְּךָ וּבְקוּמֶךָ: וּקְשַׁרְתָּם לְאוֹת עַל יָדֶךָ, וְהָיוּ לְטֹטָפֹת בֵּין עֵינֶיךָ: וּכְתַבְתָּם עַל מְזֻזוֹת בֵּיתֶךָ וּבִשְׁעָרֶיךָ:

▲ *The Shema is so important in Judaism that some parts of it are recited daily*

Torah. It was considered so important that Jews had to recite it twice a day. Reciting the Shema is sometimes described in Jewish literature as 'accepting the yoke of the Kingdom of heaven'. The second statement is taken from Leviticus:

> ❝ You shall not take vengeance or bear a grudge against any of your people, but you shall love your neighbour as yourself: I am the Lord. ❞
>
> *Leviticus* 19:18 [NRSV]

When the man agreed with Jesus, he also touched on something else close to Jesus' teaching, that keeping such commandments was more important than burnt offerings and sacrifice. Jesus was like the prophets of the eighth century BCE, who taught that justice was more important than sacrifices and empty worship (Amos 5:21–24). According to Mark, scribe accepted the view that people are more important than religious activity – especially if that activity was not combined with meeting the needs of others. Jesus recognised the wisdom of the man and told him that he was not far from the Kingdom of God.

■ Christians today

Some Christians today might think that everything Jesus did contradicted the religious leaders of the time. This passage shows that this was not the case. According to Mark, Jesus and the other religious teachers agreed with one another here. They agreed on the important message that loving God should be followed by the loving of one's neighbour.

In Luke's Gospel, Jesus was asked, 'Who is my neighbour?' He goes on to tell the story of the Good Samaritan (Luke 10:29). Mark does not include this, but leaves the reader to understand that one's 'neighbour' is anyone – Jew or Gentile. Christians believe that being a member of the Kingdom of God is not just about going to church, or following certain rules, but it is about respect for God and treatment of fellow humans.

▲ *Christians show their love for their neighbour at Christian festivals, such as Harvest Festival, during which donations are collected for those in need*

Activities

1 The Golden Rule is described as 'do to others what you would have them do to you.' Consider how close this is to Jesus' teaching here.

2 If everyone followed Jesus' teaching to the letter, would we need any other laws? If yes, what might they be? Explain your answer.

3 'Jesus' teaching on the greatest commandment is unrealistic.' Evaluate this statement, giving two points of view and a justified conclusion.

4 'Love God and do what you will.' Is this good advice for believers?

Discussion activity

Discuss these cases with your group and decide what you think would be the most loving thing to do:

a A student in your school is being bullied.

b Your friend tells you that they have been offered drugs.

⭐ Study tip

Make sure you know the differences between this story about the scribe's question and the passage about the rich man who asked what he needed to do to inherit eternal life.

Summary

You should now understand Jesus' teaching that to be a member of the Kingdom of God requires believers to love God and their neighbour.

> A leper came to him begging him, and kneeling he said to him, 'If you choose, you can make me clean.' Moved with pity, Jesus stretched out his hand and touched him, and said to him, 'I do choose. Be made clean!' Immediately the leprosy left him, and he was made clean. After sternly warning him he sent him away at once, saying to him, 'See that you say nothing to anyone; but go, show yourself to the priest, and offer for your cleansing what Moses commanded, as a testimony to them.' But he went out and began to proclaim it freely, and to spread the word, so that Jesus could no longer go into a town openly, but stayed out in the country; and people came to him from every quarter.
>
> *Mark* 1:40–45 [NRSV]

Objectives

- Study the incident of the man with leprosy healed by Jesus.
- Understand the importance of the incident for Jesus' ministry, for the disciples and for people today.

■ Illness in the first century

In the time of Jesus, illness was seen to be something caused by sin. In many cases it cut you off from society, and if you fell ill or were disabled, you were rejected by others. This was particularly true of skin diseases, especially leprosy. Lepers were expected not to touch anyone or approach anyone nearer than 50 paces, for fear that they would pass on the disease or make the other person 'unclean' spiritually.

■ The man's faith

This incident is at the beginning of Mark's Gospel. Jesus had begun to preach and teach in Galilee and had already healed many people. The man had leprosy and therefore would have been made to live outside the village. His request was clear – he wanted to be made clean. Cleanliness was very important in first-century Judaism. If people became unclean by illness or touching dead bodies, they could not participate in worship. Here the man, who approached Jesus on his knees, was careful not to touch Jesus.

■ Jesus' response

The text notes that Jesus 'was moved with pity'. Jesus was perhaps indignant about the situation of lepers. They had fallen ill and had been rejected by their society, and so their suffering was made even worse. Jesus touched the man. Mark does not mention the reaction of those there, but it is likely that they would have been shocked. Jesus

Research activities

1 Look up Leviticus 13:1–8 and 14:1–9 to see some of the rules in the Bible about leprosy.

2 Visit The Leprosy Mission website to learn more about how leprosy affects people today, and how this Christian organisation offers help to those suffering from leprosy.

▲ *Even today there are people in the world living with leprosy*

was making himself ritually unclean by this action. For Jesus this did not matter; the man's needs were what mattered.

There is a glimpse of the Messianic Secret in this passage – the man was told to tell no one, but he ignored this. He was also told to go to the priests to be declared clean from leprosy, in order to fulfil a requirement in Jewish law. On the rare occasions that people did recover from skin diseases and leprosy they could be declared clean. There was a complex ritual for this, involving sacrifice, and the priest could issue a written bill of health when all the checks were done.

According to Mark, Jesus not only healed the man, but also made sure that he would be able to take part in society again. Jesus showed his commitment to the outcast and the rejected. He also demonstrated that things could be changed and a different approach was necessary, showing love and care.

Notice the last sentence, which is typical of Mark's Gospel. It says, 'people came from everywhere' to find Jesus. Here Mark shows the impact of this cure on those who heard about it.

■ Leprosy today

Leprosy is still a problem in the world today. It is an infectious disease that affects people in poverty. Yet it can be cured for very little money. The Leprosy Mission is an international Christian organisation that exists to support and help those who suffer from leprosy around the world. Those who work for the Mission offer healthcare, rehabilitation, education and training, small business loans, housing, fresh water supplies and sanitation. Their aim is not only to heal those with leprosy, but to get rid of the social stigma that still exists around leprosy. People still become social outcasts as a result of skin diseases, including leprosy.

Links

See pages 10–11 for more on the Messianic Secret.

Discussion activity

Which groups of people are treated as outcasts in society today? What do you think Christian believers should do for them?

Activities

1 Explain why Dr Thomas' actions reflect Jesus' example in supporting those rejected by society.

2 'No one should ever be made to live as an outcast today.' Do you agree? Give reasons for your answer.

Dr M. A. Thomas

Dr M. A. Thomas worked as a Christian preacher and evangelist in Rajasthan, India. He worked with the poorest in society, in particular the lowest caste in India, the *Dalits*. His work led him to found churches and Sunday schools for the poor. In 1978 he went to a leper colony in Faridabad, Delhi. He had no money with which to help the lepers. He wrote, 'I shook hands with the lepers who even had pus on their hands. I have never seen another person shaking hands with the lepers.' He raised money to support them and in 1978 brought 26 children from the leper colony to his orphanage. The children of these lepers did not have leprosy. The charity that he founded, Hopegivers, now helps hundreds of leper colonies. He died in 2010 but his work continues. (www.hopegivers.org)

▲ *Dr M. A. Thomas founded a charity that helps people suffering from leprosy*

Summary

You have now studied the healing of the man with leprosy and Jesus' willingness to touch him and cure him. You have also learnt that there is a long-term Christian commitment to meeting the needs of those with leprosy.

★ Study tip

Remember that Christians help many types of people who feel rejected by society.

> " Jesus went out again beside the lake; the whole crowd gathered around him, and he taught them. As he was walking along, he saw Levi son of Alphaeus sitting at the tax booth, and he said to him, 'Follow me.' And he got up and followed him.
>
> And as he sat at dinner in Levi's house, many tax-collectors and sinners were also sitting with Jesus and his disciples—for there were many who followed him. When the scribes of the Pharisees saw that he was eating with sinners and tax-collectors, they said to his disciples, 'Why does he eat with tax-collectors and sinners?' When Jesus heard this, he said to them, 'Those who are well have no need of a physician, but those who are sick; I have come to call not the righteous but sinners.' "
>
> *Mark* 2:13–17 [NRSV]

Objective

- Understand the importance of the call of Levi as an event in Jesus' ministry and as an example of Jesus engaging with social outcasts.

Key term

- **tax collectors:** Jewish men who collected taxes on behalf of the Romans

Links

See page 76–77 for more on the call of the first disciples.

Jesus needed a close group of followers to support his work. It was common for teachers in the first century to have a group of followers. Many young men would have wanted to be disciples of a religious teacher like Jesus. However in this incident Jesus would have shocked those around him. A **tax collector** would not have been a likely candidate for such discipleship.

■ Tax collectors

As a group in first-century Palestine, the tax collectors were among the most hated. They were Jews who worked for the Romans collecting Roman taxes. They also had a reputation for charging more than was necessary and ensuring that they had a good lifestyle. There were two types of taxes in Palestine at the time. One was for the upkeep of the Temple, which all were expected to pay, and the other was the Roman taxation. The tax collectors dealt with the latter. In that part of Galilee, Levi would have been working for Herod Antipas, the Jewish ruler of Galilee who only ruled because the Romans allowed him to.

■ Levi, Son of Alphaeus

It is not clear who Alphaeus was, but Levi was a common name. Levi responded immediately to Jesus' call – he left his tax booth and followed Jesus. Later tradition has identified Levi with Matthew, the author of Matthew's Gospel. Matthew is described as a tax collector (Matthew 9:9–10) and, as these passages are almost identical, it is generally accepted that they are the same person.

▲ *The call of Levi is depicted in this painting by James Jacques Jospeh Tissot*

■ Jesus criticised

There are few things more sociable than eating a meal with friends. Jesus is described as eating with tax collectors and sinners. The Pharisees would have seen this as unacceptable. How could this man associate with such people? In the Pharisees' view, people like tax collectors were not following the religious teachings of the day, as they did not keep the detail of the law.

Jesus' response was clear. He said, 'Those who are well have no need of a physician, but those who are sick; I have come to call not the righteous but sinners.' In the Old Testament tradition 'sinners' were regarded as 'wicked'. They did not just break the law – they lived outside it. There is no indication in this passage from Mark that Jesus expected them to change their lives, but in parallel passages (e.g. Zacchaeus in Luke 19:1–10) there is evidence of a change in lifestyle.

Jesus was challenging the Pharisees here. They saw themselves as keepers and teachers of the law. Yet there were groups of people that they would not engage with. Jesus did engage with these groups. He believed that by demonstrating love and care for the people, they would hear his message and could enter the Kingdom of God. The beginnings of a conflict between Jesus and the Pharisees and other teachers of the law can be seen in this passage.

■ Implications for Christians in society today

This incident demonstrates the importance of Jesus' mission to those who were outcasts. He was showing in actions and words that the love of God is for all. Christians today work with outcasts and those on the fringes of society. All forms of Christian work with people are about offering God's forgiveness and then trying to support people to work and live with integrity and as disciples of Jesus.

▲ Christian charities like the Salvation Army serve meals to the homeless and people living in food poverty

Summary

You should now know that Jesus had a tax collector among his disciples and this was a sign of God's acceptance of those rejected by society.

> 66 From there he set out and went away to the region of Tyre. He entered a house and did not want anyone to know he was there. Yet he could not escape notice, but a woman whose little daughter had an unclean spirit immediately heard about him, and she came and bowed down at his feet. Now the woman was a Gentile, of Syrophoenician origin. She begged him to cast the demon out of her daughter. He said to her, 'Let the children be fed first, for it is not fair to take the children's food and throw it to the dogs.' But she answered him, 'Sir, even the dogs under the table eat the children's crumbs.' Then he said to her, 'For saying that, you may go—the demon has left your daughter.' So she went home, found the child lying on the bed, and the demon gone. 99
>
> *Mark 7:24–30* [NRSV]

Objectives

- Study the incident of the Greek (Syro-Phoenician) woman's daughter.
- Consider its importance in understanding Jesus' ministry to Gentiles and to Christians today.

Links

See page 86–87 for more on Jesus' preparation of the disciples for the mission after his death.

■ The conversation between Jesus and the woman

It is possible that Jesus had gone to Tyre to escape attention, but the woman came to find Jesus in the belief that he could cure her daughter. It was not proper for a woman to approach a strange man and have a conversation with him. However, in this case, the woman was desperate that her daughter should be healed. Mark indicates this by his use of the word 'begged', which is far stronger than merely asking.

Jesus' answer would have disappointed her. His reference to the 'children' meant the Jews. Jesus knew that his mission was to the Jews first, then to the Gentiles, the non-Jews. He must have realised that he had limited time, and that one person cannot cover the whole world. He was also aware that he was developing and training his disciples to carry on the mission after his death and resurrection. The 'food' referred to means Jesus' teaching which gives spiritual nourishment. The 'dogs' is a reference to Gentiles – Jesus was not calling the woman an unkind name. Nevertheless, in the Old Testament, dogs were regarded as unclean, because they were scavengers; they might, for example, eat meat from dead animals. It was widely believed that Jews should not mix with Gentiles because they might lead them away from God and his laws.

The woman was persistent. Just as Bartimaeus would not be quiet when Jesus was passing by, the woman responded with a remark which was at once very witty but also in some ways put herself down. When she said, 'even the dogs under the table eat the children's crumbs', she accepted Jesus' remark but demanded that she should have a share now – her daughter could be healed. Jesus was impressed by her answer, her logic and quick-wittedness. Her belief in his power led Jesus to pronounce her daughter cured.

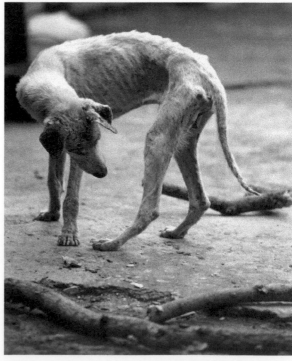

▲ *The Syro-Phoenician woman uses Jesus' metaphor of a dog to gain his sympathy: 'even the dogs under the table eat the children's crumbs.'*

■ Distance healings

This is an example of healing at a distance. Her daughter was healed of whatever illness she had (possibly a form of epilepsy). The cure was instantaneous and complete.

This is the only healing at a distance in Mark's Gospel. In this miracle the authority of Jesus is evident. He only needed to say the words and the child was healed. In Christian belief, the power of God's word begins with the creation narratives in Genesis 1. The whole of the universe and life are created when God uses the words 'let there be ...':

> **❝** Then God said, 'Let there be light'; and there was light. **❞**
>
> *Genesis* 1:3 [NRSV]

For persecuted Christians in the first century, it was a reminder that Jesus' power was with them and there was hope. It was also a reminder to the early Christians, many of whom were Gentiles, that everyone is valued by God and should be treated equally.

■ Significance for Christians today

Today's world is divided in many ways. There are those who look down on others, and there are many who feel discriminated against. Discrimination means to treat people differently, very often badly, for reasons of prejudice based on things that people cannot control, e.g. upbringing, ethnic origin, skin colour, sexual orientation and gender. People who are pre-judged and treated differently in this way feel that other people are against them. In this passage there is a clear message to Christians that they should not prejudge and should not discriminate. Jesus could have discriminated against the woman because she was foreign and female, but he did not and her daughter was healed. This sets an example for Christians to follow: they should value everyone equally and not discriminate against anyone.

After Jesus' death, the disciples began to preach to all who would hear them, Jews and Gentiles. As Christianity spread, people of different races and backgrounds from Europe, Asia and Africa became Christians. Today, Christianity includes people from all over the world. Paul, who wrote many letters to the early Christians, expressed the beliefs of those who followed Jesus that, 'There is no longer Jew or Greek, there is no longer slave or free, there is no longer male and female; for all of you are one in Christ Jesus.' (Galatians 3:28)

Activities

1 Compare this story with that of the healing of Jairus' daughter (Mark 5:21–24a, 35–43). What are the similarities and differences? What does each teach about Jesus' authority?

2 'This woman understood Jesus' mission better than the disciples did.' Evaluate this statement and explain what you think. Refer to Mark's Gospel in your answer.

Extension activity

Read Genesis 1:1–2:4 to see the way in which the word of God is powerful. Compare that to John 1:1–4 which refers to Jesus as 'the Word'. Notice that these images are not used in Mark's Gospel, where it is the words that Jesus speaks which bring about God's activity.

Key terms

● **prejudice:** unfairly judging someone before the facts are known; holding biased opinions about an individual or group

● **discrimination:** actions or behaviour that result from prejudice

Research activity

Look up the Prayer of Humble Access, in many Holy Communion services, and see how the woman's words continue to be used today.

⭐ Study tip

Remember that Jesus' attitude to women and Gentiles was unlike that of many people of his time.

Summary

You should now understand the healing of the Greek (Syro-Phoenician) woman's daughter. You should understand what it means for Christian believers and their understanding of Jesus' mission and his authority.

> ❝ When they came to the disciples, they saw a great crowd around them, and some scribes arguing with them. When the whole crowd saw him, they were immediately overcome with awe, and they ran forward to greet him. He asked them, 'What are you arguing about with them?' Someone from the crowd answered him, 'Teacher, I brought you my son; he has a spirit that makes him unable to speak; and whenever it seizes him, it dashes him down; and he foams and grinds his teeth and becomes rigid; and I asked your disciples to cast it out, but they could not do so.'
>
> He answered them, 'You faithless generation, how much longer must I be among you? How much longer must I put up with you? Bring him to me.' And they brought the boy to him. When the spirit saw him, immediately it threw the boy into convulsions, and he fell on the ground and rolled about, foaming at the mouth. Jesus asked the father, 'How long has this been happening to him?' And he said, 'From childhood. It has often cast him into the fire and into the water, to destroy him; but if you are able to do anything, have pity on us and help us.'
>
> Jesus said to him, 'If you are able!—All things can be done for the one who believes.' Immediately the father of the child cried out, 'I believe; help my unbelief!' When Jesus saw that a crowd came running together, he rebuked the unclean spirit, saying to it, 'You spirit that keeps this boy from speaking and hearing, I command you, come out of him, and never enter him again!' After crying out and convulsing him terribly, it came out, and the boy was like a corpse, so that most of them said, 'He is dead.' But Jesus took him by the hand and lifted him up, and he was able to stand. When he had entered the house, his disciples asked him privately, 'Why could we not cast it out?' He said to them, 'This kind can come out only through **prayer**.' ❞
>
> *Mark* 9:14–29 [NRSV]

Objective

- Study the healing of the epileptic (demon-possessed) boy and understand what the incident shows about the healing ministry of Jesus.

Key terms

- **prayer:** communicating with God, either silently or through words of praise, thanksgiving or confession, or requests for God's help or guidance
- **exorcism:** driving out evil spirits

★ Study tip

This is a long passage and it is important that you learn the details carefully.

▲ *Jesus told the disciples that only prayer could heal this kind of illness*

Mark writes that this incident began while Jesus, Peter, James and John were up the mountain of transfiguration. It is a miracle which is an example of an **exorcism**, because the people believed that the boy was possessed by an evil spirit.

■ Jesus' words

Jesus emerges from this incident as one who challenges disbelief and scepticism. Yet he also met the boy's needs by curing him and the father's needs by responding to his request.

Jesus was critical of the people around, describing them as a 'faithless generation'. It is possible that this was directed at the disciples, who had failed to cure the boy because they lacked the faith, or at the father of the possessed boy. He certainly responded quickly to the father when he said, 'if you are able.'

Jesus' authority is clear. Mark uses the word 'command' to describe when Jesus ordered the spirit out of the boy. This leaves no room for doubt that Mark believed that God's power was at work.

■ The crowd

The crowd had clearly missed Jesus when he was up the mountain, because when he reappeared, they greeted him warmly. This is probably because the people believed that where the disciples had failed, Jesus would succeed.

■ The disciples' question

The disciples were obviously concerned that they had tried and failed to heal the boy. They waited until they were alone with Jesus and asked him why. Jesus taught them that prayer was an essential part of the healing.

■ Prayer and miracles

Prayer is often linked to miracles. In Mark's Gospel, Jesus is depicted as praying on a number of occasions (most notably in Gethsemane). Prayer is a way that humans try to communicate with God in silence, words and actions. Prayer was an important part of synagogue worship for

▲ *William Temple, who was Archbishop of Canterbury from 1942 to 1944, was once challenged on the existence of miracles*

Jews, and so the Jewish tradition of prayer would have been well known to the disciples. They believed that God answered prayer, not necessarily providing all that had been asked, but listening to their needs and responding to them. So Jesus prayed to God in Gethsemane, 'yet, not what I want, but what you want' (Mark 14:36).

Within Jesus' teaching though, there was a different aspect to prayer. The relationship that Jesus had with God was so close that he could use the word 'Abba' (Dad). The disciples had yet to discover this. Later when Jesus was teaching his disciples he said, 'So I tell you, whatever you ask for in prayer, believe that you have received it, and it will be yours.' (Mark 11:24)

Most modern miraculous cures are linked to prayer. Many churches hold healing services to pray for the sick and to lay hands on those who are sick. In Christian tradition there are places of prayer and worship which are linked with the sick, for example, Lourdes in France.

Activity

William Temple, a former Archbishop of Canterbury, was once told that answers to prayer were coincidence. He replied, 'That may be true, but I've noticed that when I pray coincidences happen and when I don't, they don't.' What do you think of Archbishop Temple's remarks?

Research activity

Find out about Lourdes and the ministry to the sick that takes place there.

Summary

You should have now studied a miracle which is an exorcism and should understand the importance of prayer in healing.

Activities

1 Was the man praying when he brought his son to Jesus?
2 When do you think people are most likely to pray?
3 'If prayer does not seem to be answered, does that mean that God does not care?' What do you think? Give reasons to support your answer.

The widow at the treasury – Mark 12:41–44

> ❝ He sat down opposite the treasury, and watched the crowd putting money into the treasury. Many rich people put in large sums. A poor widow came and put in two small copper coins, which are worth a penny. Then he called his disciples and said to them, 'Truly I tell you, this poor widow has put in more than all those who are contributing to the treasury. For all of them have contributed out of their abundance; but she out of her poverty has put in everything she had, all she had to live on.' ❞
>
> *Mark* 12:41–44 [NRSV]

There were many rules about the way that widows should be treated in the Old Testament. People knew that widows had little after their husbands had died, so they should have been protected from those who wanted to mistreat them. Nevertheless for many widows, poverty was a way of life.

This incident gave Jesus the chance to teach his disciples about the nature of generosity. The widow gave a small amount, which many would have looked down on. But Jesus' teaching shows that it is not the amount that you give, but the proportion of your wealth and the level of sacrifice that is important.

■ The Temple

The Temple in Jerusalem was originally built by King Solomon to house the Ark of the Covenant, which contained the Ten Commandments. It was the centre of Jewish worship. The Temple was the only place where Jewish priests made sacrifices to God. The people believed that God resided there. For Jews, the Temple was the most important building in the world. It had been rebuilt after 20 BCE, during the reign of Herod the Great.

It was also a place of great wealth. People had always given money and possessions to the Temple, and the vessels used in the Temple were made of the finest gold and silver. The robes that the priests wore and the curtains were made of the best material. There were warehouses attached to the Temple which stored wine and corn. Some of the money given to the Temple was used to pay the priests.

The treasury was in the Court of Women. The various courts of the Temple were created to give different people access. The Court of Women allowed women and children into the Temple area.

Objective

- Understand the incident of the widow at the treasury and its meaning for Christians.

Research activity

Read the story of Ruth in the Old Testament (Ruth 1–4) and reflect on how she was treated. There is a link between Ruth and Jesus – what is it?

▲ *The Western Wall, the only remaining part of the buildings connected with Herod's Temple*

■ The woman's gift

The woman's gift was a small amount. The coins that she deposited were 'lepta' coins, the smallest value coins at the time. The priests examined the coins and announced what had been given. The widow's offering would not have been secret, and this would have left her open to ridicule. Her offering, though, was very great compared to the offerings of rich people. They just gave a bit of their wealth, and she gave all the money she had.

■ Jesus' praise

According to Mark, Jesus praised the woman for her generous spirit. She did not just give small change because it was easy, but because she did not have anything else to give. She was showing great faith and commitment. She did not give in order to be praised, but out of her love for God. Just as the woman who anointed Jesus' feet at Bethany used expensive perfume (Mark 14:1–9), the widow gave more than she could afford.

The woman in this passage is like the disciples. When Jesus called them, they gave up everything they had. When Jesus met the rich man he challenged him to give everything up as a mark of discipleship, but the rich man couldn't do this.

■ The message for Christians today

The need to be generous is part of the Christian way of life today. Sacrificial generosity like the woman showed is not always common. There is a parallel between this woman, who gave all that she had, and Jesus, who was prepared to sacrifice his life to save humanity from their sins.

This incident is another example of Jesus aligning himself with someone who was on the fringes of society; the widow was praised – the rich were not.

Links

The story of the woman who anointed Jesus at Bethany (Mark 14:1–9) is introduced on the next page.

Activities

1 Should all donations to charity be given anonymously? Explain the reasons for your answer.

2 If a benefactor gives money on condition that they receive publicity, should the donation be refused? Give reasons for your answer.

3 'Rich Christians are not good Christians.' Evaluate this statement in the light of the texts that you have studied in Mark's Gospel.

David Green

David Green is an American billionaire. He believes that his $3 billion fortune does not belong to him but to God. He gives his money away to support the Christian Church. He said that it is impossible to separate church life and work life. 'You can't have a belief system on Sunday and not live it the other six days.' While David has not given everything away, he believes in massive generosity in proportion to his wealth. It is estimated that he has given away over $500 million.

▲ David Green has donated much of his wealth to the Church

★ Study tip

Remember that this passage teaches Christians that it is not how much they give that is important, but the level of sacrifice that they make.

Summary

You should now understand Jesus' teaching about the nature of generosity – it is not important how much you give but how much sacrifice it entails.

The anointing at Bethany – Mark 14:1–9

> " It was two days before the Passover and the Festival of Unleavened Bread. The chief priests and the scribes were looking for a way to arrest Jesus by stealth and kill him; for they said, 'Not during the festival, or there may be a riot among the people.'
>
> While he was at Bethany in the house of Simon the leper, as he sat at the table, a woman came with an alabaster jar of very costly ointment of nard, and she broke open the jar and poured the ointment on his head. But some were there who said to one another in anger, 'Why was the ointment wasted in this way? For this ointment could have been sold for more than three hundred denarii, and the money given to the poor.' And they scolded her. But Jesus said, 'Let her alone; why do you trouble her? She has performed a good service for me. For you always have the poor with you, and you can show kindness to them whenever you wish; but you will not always have me. She has done what she could; she has anointed my body beforehand for its burial. Truly I tell you, wherever the good news is proclaimed in the whole world, what she has done will be told in remembrance of her.' "
>
> *Mark* 14:1–9 [NRSV]

Objective

- Study the incident of the anointing at Bethany and its meaning.

Key terms

- **universalism:** the belief that God's Kingdom is for all, including those looked down on by others
- **anoint:** to put oil on the head to show that God has chosen a person

According to Mark, this incident occurred just before Jesus was arrested. He was in Bethany, just outside Jerusalem, at the home of Simon. Simon had been cured of leprosy, but had kept the nickname 'the leper'.

■ The plot against Jesus

At the start of this passage the chief priests wanted to arrest Jesus, and have him tried and crucified. They feared that Jesus might be arrested during the Festival of Unleavened Bread when Jerusalem was full of visitors and so there could be trouble. Many pilgrims travelled to Jerusalem for the Festival of Unleavened Bread, which started with the Passover celebration.

■ The woman's actions and their importance

Anointing was an action full of symbolism:

- Kings were anointed in the Old Testament as a mark of their authority from God
- The Messiah (Christ) was the 'anointed one'
- Anyone who was buried was anointed as part of the burial ritual
- Visitors would sometimes be anointed as an act of hospitality and a sign of respect.

There is a big contrast between the woman's action and Simon's behaviour. She treated Jesus with great respect, while Simon did not. Honoured guests and visitors at Jewish houses should have been anointed with oil, but the text suggests that Simon did not do this.

▲ *A glass perfume bottle from the 1st Century BCE; perfume the woman used was valuable, which shows her respect for Jesus*

Jesus' praise for the woman is very important. She is described as preparing Jesus for burial and that 'wherever the good news is proclaimed in the whole world, what she has done will be told in remembrance of her.' She set an example to Christians of sacrificial giving and of commitment.

■ Criticism of the woman

Mark does not tell us who spoke harshly to the woman for wasting the perfume. The statement that it was worth 'more than three hundred denarii' may well be an exaggeration for effect, but it shows it was considered valuable.

Jesus did not think the woman should be criticised, and again had to point out that she had understood what was going to happen to him, while they had not. They had focused on the value of the perfume and not the symbolism of her action.

■ Importance for Christians today

'You always have the poor with you, and you can show kindness to them whenever you wish.' This saying of Jesus sums up his teaching. He recognised that poverty would always exist and that if the disciples were concerned about it they should do something about it. Here, once more, Jesus met someone who was outside society. Simon, as a cured leper, would have experienced being outside society. The unnamed woman was not part of the meal and was treated as an outsider by those who criticised her.

For Christians today the key phrase is that the woman did 'what she could'. The Christian Church teaches that Christians should do what they can, when they can, to meet the needs of those who are on the edge of, or outside, society and in need. Christians have a belief in universalism, in the sense that the message of the Gospel is open to all people. This is based on the Old Testament idea that one day everyone will be part of God's Kingdom. Jesus followed this here and showed his commitment to God's Kingdom being open to all.

▲ Poor children from Guatemala, South America; 'You always have the poor with you, and you can show kindness to them whenever you wish' (Mark 14: 7)

Activities

1 Explain how Mark contrasts the plot against Jesus with the actions of the woman.

2 Were those who criticised the woman correct to do so? Give reasons for your answer.

3 Which groups of people are disregarded by society today? Make a list. What could Christians do for them based on the example of Jesus?

4 'Mark wanted to show that Jesus had good news for everyone.' Evaluate this statement, showing that you have thought about more than one point of view. Refer to Mark's Gospel in your answer.

Research activity 🔍

Find out about the work of Sally Trench and how she helped the homeless.

⭐ Study tip

There are other versions of this story in Matthew, Luke and John. It is important that you focus on learning the version in Mark's Gospel.

Summary

You should now know the story of the woman who anointed Jesus at Bethany and its importance for those who were there and for Christians today.

6 Faith and discipleship

6.1 The call of the first disciples – Mark 1:16–20

> **"** As Jesus passed along the Sea of Galilee, he saw Simon and his brother Andrew casting a net into the sea—for they were fishermen. And Jesus said to them, 'Follow me and I will make you fish for people.' And immediately they left their nets and followed him. As he went a little farther, he saw James son of Zebedee and his brother John, who were in their boat mending the nets. Immediately he called them; and they left their father Zebedee in the boat with the hired men, and followed him. **"**
>
> *Mark* 1:16–20 [NRSV]

Objective

● Study the **call** of the first **disciples** and understand what it teaches about Christian discipleship.

Key terms

● **call:** the feeling that a person has to follow a particular lifestyle or career, very often linked to service (see also 'vocation' on page xx)

● **disciple:** the term used for the followers of Jesus

The region of Galilee where Jesus grew up is to the north-west of the Sea of Galilee, which provides water and fish for this area. Fishing was a common occupation around the Sea of Galilee. However, it is interesting that the first disciples Jesus called were fishermen.

■ Jesus' call

Jesus does not seem to have had a conversation with Simon and Andrew. He just said the words, 'follow me'. Their reaction was instant. Jesus said that he would send them out to fish for people. This is a reference to the mission that the disciples were embarking on – they were to serve in spreading the news of the Kingdom of God. Later Jesus renamed Simon as Peter.

Jesus then went on to call James and his brother John, sons of Zebedee. The fact that they had hired men meant that they were reasonably wealthy, and perhaps had more to lose in following Jesus. It is interesting that their relative wealth did not prevent Jesus from calling them.

In both cases Mark writes that they left their nets, workplace, fellow workers and family instantly and followed Jesus. At this stage Jesus does not seem to have promised them anything in return for their sacrifice. Jewish teachers often had groups of disciples with them, so Jesus was doing what many other rabbis did at the time. However, there is no record of others 'calling' disciples like Jesus did. We do not know the reason for the disciples' decision to follow Jesus. Perhaps they already knew Jesus and trusted him, or perhaps his teaching inspired them. They were clearly impressed by Jesus at first sight and may have heard something of him in Galilee already.

▲ *Fishing on the Sea of Galilee still happens today*

■ The disciples

A disciple is a 'learner' and a 'follower'. The disciples were expected to follow Jesus and learn from his teachings and actions. There was an expectation that disciples would continue the work of the master after he had left them or died.

The disciples could not have known what they were committing to at the time. They were to spend about three years with Jesus and then witness the end of his life and his resurrection.

■ What can modern Christians learn from the call of the disciples?

The disciples did not hesitate when called. Christians today sometimes make a commitment to their belief instantly, inspired by the teaching of the Bible, a preacher or the experience of others. The first disciples left behind their possessions and family. While this is not expected of all Christian followers today, there are a large number who dedicate their whole life to following Jesus. Monks, nuns and some priests take vows of poverty, chastity and obedience, such is their commitment to Christianity. For others who continue with their daily lives, their faith affects the way they live and work with people and changes their priorities.

There is an unquestioning aspect to the call of the disciples and, while Christians are encouraged to learn about their faith and debate issues, the initial commitment is made without question. The disciples were chosen because Jesus recognised in them an ability to show commitment, and modern disciples may be expected to do the same. Christians sometimes may have questions, doubts and concerns, but their commitment helps and encourages them.

The disciples became a community around Jesus. Christianity is a communal religion. Modern Christians join together for worship and other activities. They believe that this strengthens their faith and supports them in their discipleship.

Bishop Hugh Montefiore

Bishop Hugh was born of Jewish parents. One day, at the age of 16, while sitting in his study, he saw an apparition – a figure in white coming towards him, saying, 'Follow me.' Montefiore later said that the figure he saw was that of Jesus, and that his conversion was simple and immediate, and he has never looked back. He went on to become a priest in the Church of England, and became Bishop of Birmingham. There was a sacrifice for Montefiore though – he became separated from his family and community. He said, 'For a Jew to become a Christian is to go over to the enemy.' Montefiore chose to make a commitment to Christianity despite the sacrifice he knew it would involve.

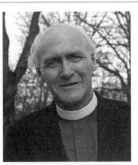

▲ Bishop Montefiore was also a writer of books about Christianity

> 66 And a large crowd followed him and pressed in on him. Now there was a woman who had been suffering from haemorrhages for twelve years. She had endured much under many physicians, and had spent all that she had; and she was no better, but rather grew worse. She had heard about Jesus, and came up behind him in the crowd and touched his cloak, for she said, 'If I but touch his clothes, I will be made well.' Immediately her haemorrhage stopped; and she felt in her body that she was healed of her disease.
>
> Immediately aware that power had gone forth from him, Jesus turned about in the crowd and said, 'Who touched my clothes?' And his disciples said to him, 'You see the crowd pressing in on you; how can you say, "Who touched me?"' He looked all around to see who had done it. But the woman, knowing what had happened to her, came in fear and trembling, fell down before him, and told him the whole truth. He said to her, 'Daughter, your faith has made you well; go in peace, and be healed of your disease.' 99
>
> *Mark 5:24b–34* [NRSV]

Objective

- Study the healing of the woman with haemorrhages and what it teaches about faith.

Key term

- **haemorrhage:** bleeding which is persistent and potentially life threatening

Links

See pages 64–65 for more on the healing of the man with leprosy (Mark 1:40–45).

■ The woman's faith

In first-century Palestine, the woman would have been rejected by society. She had an illness that almost certainly would have prevented her from working and living a normal family life. She had tried the medical treatments of the day but was still ill. She would have been classed as unclean, yet Jesus was not angry with her for touching him. Her faith was captured by Mark when he recorded the words, 'If I but touch his clothes, I will be made well.' There was a clear recognition that Jesus' authority included the power to heal without knowing the person who needed healing, or even that she was there.

The cure was instant and yet her faith almost failed when Jesus asked who had touched him. She became frightened and fell at his feet. In contrast to the man who knelt before him to be cured of leprosy, she had no choice but to tell Jesus what she had done.

▲ *This painting by William Blake, from 1808, depicts the woman reaching to touch Jesus' clothes; this incident connects faith with healing*

■ The disciples

According to Mark, the disciples did not realise what was happening. When Jesus asked who had touched him, they saw the crowd and wondered how Jesus could ask such a question. They were unaware of the feeling that Jesus must have had when 'power had gone forth from him'. The early Christians, being persecuted in Rome, would have learned from this that discipleship means faith. The twelve had demonstrated their faith in following Jesus immediately and staying with him. This woman had shown great faith, even though she was not a disciple.

■ Jesus' teaching

Jesus praised the woman for her faith. He gave her spiritual comfort by telling her to go in peace and that she would continue to be free from suffering. This was not a hope, but a clear statement. Jesus knew that his healings were complete and permanent, and involved both physical and spiritual healing.

In telling the woman to go in peace, Jesus would have used the word 'shalom'. This word means not just wellbeing, but inner peace. The use of shalom was also an indication that he was a peaceful Messiah.

Jesus called the woman 'daughter'. This is a term of endearment and shows that Jesus not only accepted her faith, but treated her well as a person. He was demonstrating the equality of every person in the eyes of God, and his approach to her would have seemed unusually kind and considerate to those around him.

■ What can modern Christians learn from the woman with a haemorrhage?

Modern Christians can learn to have faith. One of the changes from Jesus' time to the present is that many people have faith, but only in the things that they can prove. The idea of touching someone's clothes to be cured would be odd to them. They rely on the science of medicine, although doctors themselves are often aware that their patient's state of mind is important in the healing process. Their 'faith' lies in the belief that the doctors' scientific medicine will cure them. Many Christians today do not question that Jesus could heal through faith, and there are many Christians who exercise a ministry of healing through faith. They do not dismiss the science of medicine, but believe that they can add to its effectiveness.

▲ *Lourdes is believed by many Christians today to be a place of healing*

Activity

Imagine you were one of the disciples telling someone afterwards what had happened. How would you explain your reaction to Jesus' question, 'Who touched my clothes?'

Discussion activity

Discuss in groups whether it was the woman's faith that made her well or Jesus' (God's) power.

Research activity

Study the life of Helen Keller. How did she use her faith to improve the lives of others who were blind?

⭐ Study tip

It is important to learn the detail of stories like this accurately so that you can use them in longer answers to illustrate any discussion about faith and healing.

Summary

You have now studied a miracle that demonstrates the link between faith and healing. You should understand that it demonstrates Jesus' treatment of everyone as equal in God's eyes.

> **"** He called **the Twelve** and began to send them out two by two, and gave them authority over the unclean spirits. He ordered them to take nothing for their journey except a staff; no bread, no bag, no money in their belts; but to wear sandals and not to put on two tunics. He said to them, 'Wherever you enter a house, stay there until you leave the place. If any place will not welcome you and they refuse to hear you, as you leave, shake off the dust that is on your feet as a testimony against them.' So they went out and proclaimed that all should repent. They cast out many demons, and **anointed** with oil many who were sick and cured them. **"**
>
> *Mark* 6:7–13 [NRSV]

Discipleship had to be, and still is, an active life. It was not enough for the disciples to follow Jesus, watch his actions and listen to his teachings. Jesus needed them to continue his mission after he had ascended into heaven. The disciples had to be trained and given experience of what such work would mean. Their backgrounds were diverse, and it is not likely that any of them had been religious leaders or teachers before they had met Jesus. Jesus then sent them on a mission with minimum equipment, but very clear instructions.

■ Jesus' instructions

Jesus gave the disciples several clear instructions:

- They must take a staff. Walking any distance is helped by a staff. It would also act as protection against anything that threatened them. The idea of using a staff is similar to a shepherd's crook, and today when bishops take part in ceremonies they carry a crozier, which looks like a shepherd's crook.

- They should take no bread, bag or money. They were to rely on faith and the generosity of others. They had to believe that God would provide for them.

- They should wear sandals, but take only one shirt. They were expected to travel light. Sandals were essential in those days on the poor paths and tracks that they would have followed.

- They must stay in the same house that welcomed them. Elijah had stayed in the widow of Zarephath's house for some time, and God provided for the widow, her son and Elijah (1 Kings 17). This was a model for them.

- They should shake the dust off their feet if a place would not accept them. This was a symbolic act and equivalent to separating themselves from a place that rejected their message. It was traditional if a Jewish person left Palestine to brush off their feet on their return, to prevent foreign dust contaminating the land.

Objective

- Know and understand the mission of the twelve when sent out by Jesus.

Key terms

- **the Twelve:** the group of Jesus' closest disciples
- **anoint:** to put oil on the head to show that God has chosen a person
- **exorcism:** driving out evil spirits

Activity

'It would be better to work to solve social problems than to preach the Gospel.' Evaluate this statement in the light of what you understand of Mark's Gospel.

▲ *A bishop's crozier shows that, just as Jesus is seen as the good shepherd, they too are there to care for and protect people*

■ The disciples' actions

The disciples did three things:

- They preached repentance. The people needed to be told to be sorry for the past and change their ways.

- They drove out demons. The Jews believed that illness was caused by being possessed by demons. The disciples were clearly powerful because they could perform **exorcisms**.

- They anointed with oil and healed the sick. Anointing with oil was common at that time for many reasons. Some Christians still use anointing with oil in a sacrament for those who are sick, or who are near to death. Anointing the sick with oil is only mentioned twice in the New Testament – here and in James 5:14.

This episode in the Gospel shows how far the twelve disciples were prepared to go to support the ministry of Jesus. They set out in twos, perhaps for protection, company or because of the Jewish tradition that two witnesses were needed to testify to the truth. They demonstrated faith by following Jesus' commands. They also showed their faith that God would provide for them by taking very little.

■ Christian mission today

Christians do not necessarily go out in the way that the twelve did. However they do see the need to spread the good news about Jesus. Christians today see themselves on a mission. They worship and try to live a Christian life within society. They donate to Christian charities and try to promote people's wellbeing. Many visit the sick and those in prison. Others devote themselves to the religious life and become ministers, priests, pastors or nuns. Some become missionaries and work to preach the Gospel, teach, heal, or support projects in many parts of the world. Sometimes this puts them at great risk.

Eric Liddell (1902–1945)

Eric Liddell was an Olympic athlete. He became famous for refusing to run on a Sunday because of his faith. In 1924 he won the gold medal at the Olympic Games for the 400 metres race. He was the son of missionaries who had worked in China, and he too became a missionary in China. He was a church minister and teacher. When World War II broke out and China was invaded by the Japanese, he sent his wife and children to Canada. He remained though, and was arrested. Even in the camp where he was imprisoned he continued to teach and preach. He died in the camp of an inoperable brain tumour. His work is continued today by the Eric Liddell Centre. (http://ericliddell.org/)

▲ *Eric Liddell had a reputation as a good Christian teacher and a very gentle man*

⭐ Study tip

Remember that Christian discipleship usually involves some kind of sacrifice or risk. It is not just having a set of beliefs.

Summary

You have now studied the mission that Jesus gave to the twelve disciples and its importance.

6.4 The costs and rewards of discipleship – Mark 8:34–38, 10:28–31

These two passages are taken from different parts of Mark's Gospel and contrast with each other. In the first, Mark writes that Jesus warned about the considerable cost of being a disciple, and was clear to his disciples that their discipleship would involve making sacrifices. In the second, Jesus promised that the disciples would be rewarded for their commitment.

■ The cost of discipleship

> **❝** He called the crowd with his disciples, and said to them, 'If any want to become my followers, let them deny themselves and take up their cross and follow me. For those who want to save their life will lose it, and those who lose their life for my sake, and for the sake of the Gospel, will save it. For what will it profit them to gain the whole world and forfeit their life? Indeed, what can they give in return for their life? Those who are ashamed of me and of my words in this adulterous and sinful generation, of them the Son of Man will also be ashamed when he comes in the glory of his Father with the holy angels.' **❞**
>
> *Mark 8:34–38* [NRSV]

At first sight this passage could look discouraging. According to Mark, Jesus said the disciples had to 'deny themselves'. He also told them to 'take up their cross and follow me'. The disciples had already done these things; they had given up their previous livelihoods and had followed him. The idea of denying themselves was emphasised in the mission Jesus gave them. Jesus warned them that they must 'take up their cross'. He had predicted that he would die, but until that point, he had not suggested that this might also happen to disciples. This is a clear reference to the crucifixion. The disciples did not know what would happen to them in the years after Jesus' crucifixion. Most of them faced suffering and hardship and finally died for their beliefs.

The rewards of discipleship shown in this passage

Life is an important theme in Jesus' teaching. He often spoke about eternal life after death. In this passage he tells the disciples that if they lost their lives through following his teachings, they would be rewarded with eternal life. This promise would have been very encouraging to those Christians being persecuted in Rome.

Belief in the afterlife was not universal in Judaism in the first century. For example, the Sadducees did not believe in life after death. Jesus was teaching the disciples that living a life of discipleship was more important than gaining material riches ('gaining the whole world'). If their priorities were wrong, there was a risk that they would not gain eternal life with God.

Objectives

- Consider Jesus' teachings on the costs and rewards of discipleship.
- Understand what Jesus' teachings might mean for disciples today.

Links

More on the mission Jesus gave the disciples (Mark 6:7–13) is on the previous pages: (80–81).

Activities

1 What did Jesus teach about the rewards of discipleship?

2 'Discipleship is too costly for twenty-first-century Christians.' Do you agree? Explain your opinion.

3 'People should be disciples because they will be rewarded for it.' Evaluate this statement, showing that you have thought about more than one point of view. Include references to Mark's Gospel in your answer.

Research activity

Find out what legends say happened to Peter, Thomas, Andrew and Bartholomew in the early Church.

This passage then refers to judgement. In the early Christian Church, there were probably people who gave up their faith as a result of persecution, just as Jesus had suggested in the Parable of the Sower. This teaching, while difficult, would have been encouraging, because Jesus was promising that those who maintained their faith would be rewarded when judgement came.

The cost of discipleship for twenty-first-century Christians

Discipleship is not always easy for Christians in the twenty-first century. The lifestyle of a committed Christian might feel at odds with those around them. They should not be too interested in gaining material possessions, and should live to serve others. In many parts of the world it is dangerous to be a Christian and persecution still occurs. Their commitment to worship and keeping Sunday special may mean that Christians have to have a job which leaves them free on Sundays. Many give their time freely to charitable work and activities. They support Christian charities with donations.

■ The rewards of discipleship

> ❝ Peter began to say to him, 'Look, we have left everything and followed you.' Jesus said, 'Truly I tell you, there is no one who has left house or brothers or sisters or mother or father or children or fields, for my sake and for the sake of the good news, who will not receive a hundredfold now in this age—houses, brothers and sisters, mothers and children, and fields, with persecutions—and in the age to come eternal life. But many who are first will be last, and the last will be first.' ❞
>
> *Mark* 10:28–31 [NRSV]

Most Christians believe that in this passage Jesus was teaching that the rewards of discipleship would include membership of the Kingdom of God, both in this life and after death.

This conversation comes after the rich young man had asked Jesus what he needed to do to gain eternal life. Jesus had taught that the rich would find it hard to enter the Kingdom of God. Peter was checking that the disciples had done the right thing. The disciples had left everything to follow Jesus – they were not rich – so surely they should be accepted into the Kingdom?

Jesus does not answer Peter's point directly here, but makes a promise that there would be rewards in this life, and then after death they would receive eternal life. In Jewish tradition a large healthy family and goods were signs of God's blessing, so it is possible that some believed that faith would earn material blessings. However Christians have usually understood these words to refer to spiritual riches or blessings. Notice that Mark includes the words 'with persecutions'. The early Church would have understood that well.

The phrase 'many who are first will be last' is about the transformation that faith in Christianity will bring. It would have appealed to the early Christians, many of whom came from the lower classes or were slaves.

▲ *Dietrich Bonhoeffer felt both the costs and rewards of discipleship*

Extension activity

Read about Dietrich Bonhoeffer, a Christian minister (1906–1945). How is his life connected with these texts in Mark's Gospel?

Links

To read about the Rich Man turn to pages 60–61.

★ Study tip

Try to memorise the details about one of the Christian disciples from the time of Jesus.

Summary

You have now considered Jesus' teaching on the costs or rewards of discipleship and its importance for Christians today.

> **❝** And Jesus said to them, 'You will all become deserters; for it is written,
>
> "I will strike the shepherd,
>
> and the sheep will be scattered."
>
> But after I am raised up, I will go before you to Galilee.' Peter said to him, 'Even though all become deserters, I will not.' Jesus said to him, 'Truly I tell you, this day, this very night, before the cock crows twice, you will deny me three times.' But he said vehemently, 'Even though I must die with you, I will not deny you.' And all of them said the same [...]
>
> While Peter was below in the courtyard, one of the servant-girls of the high priest came by. When she saw Peter warming himself, she stared at him and said, 'You also were with Jesus, the man from Nazareth.' But he denied it, saying, 'I do not know or understand what you are talking about.' And he went out into the forecourt. Then the cock crowed. And the servant-girl, on seeing him, began again to say to the bystanders, 'This man is one of them.' But again he denied it. Then after a little while the bystanders again said to Peter, 'Certainly you are one of them; for you are a Galilean.' But he began to curse, and he swore an oath, 'I do not know this man you are talking about.' At that moment the cock crowed for the second time. Then Peter remembered that Jesus had said to him, 'Before the cock crows twice, you will deny me three times.' And he broke down and wept. **❞**
>
> *Mark 14:27–31, 66–72 [NRSV]*

Objective

- Study the incident of Peter's denials and understand what it teaches about discipleship.

Activities

1 Why do you think Peter followed Jesus to the high priest's house?
2 What risks did Peter take?

Peter had become the leader of the disciples. He had been the one who first recognised Jesus as the Messiah. He was one of the three disciples who were allowed to be with Jesus when others were not (e.g. at the healing of Jairus' daughter, Mark 5:35–43). This incident is recorded by Mark, but the information must have come from Peter because he was the only one there.

■ Jesus' warning

Jesus knew what was going to happen to him. He warned the disciples that they would all 'fall away'. They would not have the courage to remain with him to the end. The shock of the arrest would be too much, and they would not be present at the trials or the suffering. Some may not have been present at the crucifixion – unlike the women followers of Jesus.

Peter said that he would remain with Jesus throughout, but Jesus knew what Peter would do. He predicted that before dawn (when the 'cock crows'), Peter would have denied him three times. Peter protested that such a thing would not happen.

▲ *The statue of St Peter at Capernaum, believed to be his hometown*

■ Peter in the courtyard

After the arrest Peter had followed Jesus to the high priest's house. The girl recognised him as one who had been with Jesus – she called Jesus 'the man from Nazareth'. Had this servant girl been in the Garden of Gethsemane and seen the arrest? Did she hear Peter speaking with a Galilean accent and make an educated guess? Her question became Peter's downfall.

When the cock crowed, Peter realised what he had done. At Jesus' most vulnerable moment not only had Peter left Jesus to his fate, but he had denied even being with him. This may have served as a warning to early Christians not to follow Peter's example but, equally, given his important status within the early Church, it may have encouraged them to persevere despite failures.

■ Discipleship and Peter

It is interesting to speculate why Peter denied knowing Jesus:

- Possibly he was afraid that he too would be arrested
- Perhaps he thought that the mission was ended now that Jesus was arrested
- His discipleship may not have been secure, despite all that had happened
- He had had the courage to follow Jesus, but he reacted like someone who was afraid and alone. There is no mention of the other disciples at this point.

For Christian believers who are trying to be disciples, there is much that they can learn from Peter's denials:

- Even the closest of Jesus' disciples could make mistakes
- It is possible to judge a situation wrongly and make an error like Peter's
- It is not possible for human beings to be perfect
- Peter's tears show that he repented for his mistake. He was later forgiven by Jesus
- Peter had the courage to follow Jesus when he was arrested, and to tell this story so that others would learn from it.

Mark does not record the incident, but later, after the resurrection, Jesus forgave Peter (John 21:15–19). He went on to become the leader of the Jerusalem Church and eventually found himself in Rome. There he led the Roman Church and is described as the first Pope. He is credited with writing the Letters of Peter in the New Testament.

▲ *Peter's body is believed to be buried directly under the high altar in St Peter's Basilica in Rome*

⭐ **Study tip**

This is a very important passage in understanding the character of Peter so you should try to learn it accurately.

Summary

You should now know the story of Peter's denial and understand its importance for early Christians and disciples today.

> Later he appeared to the eleven themselves as they were sitting at the table; and he upbraided them for their lack of faith and stubbornness, because they had not believed those who saw him after he had risen. And he said to them, 'Go into all the world and proclaim the good news to the whole creation. The one who believes and is baptised will be saved; but the one who does not believe will be condemned. And these signs will accompany those who believe: by using my name they will cast out demons; they will speak in new tongues; they will pick up snakes in their hands, and if they drink any deadly thing, it will not hurt them; they will lay their hands on the sick, and they will recover.'
>
> So then the Lord Jesus, after he had spoken to them, was taken up into heaven and sat down at the right hand of God. And they went out and proclaimed the good news everywhere, while the Lord worked with them and confirmed the message by the signs that accompanied it.
>
> *Mark 16:14–20 [NRSV]*

Objectives

- Study the commission of Jesus to the disciples and what it means for understanding discipleship.
- Study the ascension of Jesus and its meaning.

Key terms

- **commission:** the occasion after the resurrection of Jesus when he gave the disciples instructions about their future mission
- **ascension:** the event, 40 days after the resurrection, when Jesus returned to God, the Father, in heaven

Many scholars believe that the verses after Mark 16:8 were not part of the original text of Mark's Gospel. Some ancient texts do not include them. It is possible that writers in the early Church felt that the Gospel should end with a summary of the resurrection appearances of Jesus. However, whether it is or is not originally from Mark, these verses do include some teaching that relates to discipleship and the Christian mission after Jesus' resurrection and ascension.

In Mark 16:9–20 there are several appearances of Jesus after his resurrection, including this final appearance to the eleven disciples. Jesus told off the disciples for their lack of faith. This may have been because the disciples had doubted the resurrection witnesses and whether Jesus had really risen from the dead.

■ The commission

The word 'commission' shows that the work that the disciples were now to do, their mission, was work that they were undertaking on Jesus' behalf. He gave his disciples instructions about their mission and what they might expect:

- They were to go into the world and preach the Gospel 'to all creation'. Jesus had a vision of a universal Christian belief in God over the whole earth.
- People were to be baptised as believers, and there would be condemnation for those who did not believe. This is a reference to the judgement that will come at the end of time.

▲ *Mark 12: 19 describes how, after Jesus spoke to the disciples, 'he was taken up into heaven'*

- Those who believed, including the disciples, would be able to drive out demons and cure the sick. They would do this by laying hands on them. They would be able to speak in new languages. This is a reference to the Day of Pentecost, some seven weeks after Jesus' resurrection, recorded in the Acts of the Apostles (2:1–12). The Apostles (as the disciples were then called) were given the gift of the Holy Spirit to empower them. The text describes how they spoke in different languages.

- The reference to picking up snakes and drinking poison shows that they would be safe from danger; they should not be afraid.

■ The ascension of Jesus

Jesus is described as entering into heaven. The importance of this event is that Jesus had risen from the dead – he was not going to die again. He is then described as sitting at the right hand of God, the place of honour. This is the very thing he said would happen at his trial before the high priest. This image shows him as a king, with God's authority. It is a symbol of his power. Other texts in the New Testament also describe the **ascension** (Luke 24:50–53, Acts 1:9–11).

> ### Activity
>
> Does the ascension make it easier or more difficult to believe Jesus' message? Think about the different answers that might be given to this question by different believers and non-believers.

■ The mission in Christianity today

The writer of this passage makes it clear that the disciples did what Jesus asked of them. The early Church began in Jerusalem and soon spread outwards across the whole of the Middle East, Rome and North Africa. The story of that early work, and the work of Paul as a missionary, is described in the Acts of the Apostles.

Jesus had left the disciples for the last time and his authority had passed to them. They continued the mission and established groups of believers that later became the Church. Authority is still exercised by the Church. In some churches it is through bishops and clergy, in others elected leaders. Their role is to ensure that the mission is maintained and encouraged. There are disputes and disagreements within the Christian Church, but there are some very basic beliefs that they all preach. They all teach that God is the creator and sustains, that Jesus is the Son of God (Messiah/Christ), that the Holy Spirit is the power though which the work is done, and that God is present with believers now.

Modern Christians try to follow Jesus' teaching and undertake the work of the first disciples in various ways. Their discipleship includes preaching, teaching and healing. They work across the world and Christianity currently has some 2.5 billion followers.

> ### Research activity
>
> Some Christians describe themselves as 'Pentecostal'. Using a library or the Internet, find out what they believe.

> ### Extension activity
>
> Papias wrote about a follower of Christianity called Justus Barsabbas. Find out what he is said to have done and relate it to this passage.

▲ *Christians today still believe in preaching God's word*

> ### ⭐ Study tip
>
> Make sure that you know the differences between the mission of the Twelve (Mark 6:7–13) and the commission (Mark 16:14–20).

> **Summary**
>
> You have now studied the commission and the ascension and should understand the instructions Jesus gave to the disciples.

The Kingdom of God

You should now be able to:

✔ explain the term 'Kingdom of God' and the different ways in which it may be understood

✔ explain the meaning of the Parable of the Sower and what it teaches about the Kingdom of God

✔ explain what the Parables of the Growing Seed and the Mustard Seed teach about the Kingdom of God

✔ show how Jesus accepted children that were brought to him and explain the implications of this event for Christians today

✔ explain the teaching of Jesus to the rich man that riches can be a barrier to being part of the Kingdom of God

✔ explain Jesus' answer to the question, 'Which commandment is most important?'

✔ understand that the Kingdom of God is seen as a present reality and a future hope.

Jesus' relationship with those disregarded by society

You should now be able to:

✔ explain which groups of people were disregarded by society in first-century Palestine

✔ explain how Jesus cured a man of leprosy and the importance of this healing

✔ describe the call of Levi and explain why Jesus' may have called a tax collector to be a disciple

✔ explain the story of the Syro-Phoenician woman's daughter and recognise that Jesus was prepared to help women, and non-Jews

✔ explain the healing of the epileptic boy and its importance, showing that you understand that there is a link between healing, faith and prayer

✔ describe the story of the widow at the treasury and explain what Jesus taught about generosity in giving

✔ explain the importance of the anointing at Bethany

✔ understand the importance for Christians today of Jesus' attitudes to those disregarded by society.

Faith and discipleship

You should now be able to:

✔ explain the importance of the call of the first disciples for an understanding of discipleship

✔ explain what the incident of the healing of a woman with a haemorrhage shows about faith and healing

✔ describe and explain the mission of the twelve disciples

✔ explain the costs and rewards of discipleship, their significance for 21st-century Christians

✔ explain the importance of Peter's denials for him and for Christians today

✔ describe the commission Jesus gave his disciples and his ascension, and explain their importance

✔ explain differing views on the authority of Jesus' teaching and challenges to it

✔ understand different views about faith and its importance.

Sample student answer – the 4-mark question

1. Write an answer to the following question:

   Explain two similar things that Jesus taught about riches and the Kingdom of God.

   [4 marks]

2. Read the following student sample answer:

   "Jesus taught that riches would stop people getting into the Kingdom of God. When he was asked by the man how he could inherit eternal life Jesus told him to sell everything he owned and give it to the poor. The man could not do this because he was rich. Jesus went on to say that it was easier for a camel to go through the eye of a needle than for a rich person enter the Kingdom of God.

   Another time he saw a very poor widow give a very small amount to the Temple. Jesus praised her because she had given everything she had. Although Jesus does not say that she would enter the Kingdom of God, he was clearly teaching that generosity is important in the believer's life, so to have riches is not essential."

3. With a partner discuss the sample answer. Is the focus of the answer correct? Is anything missing from the answer? How do you think it could be improved?

4. What mark (out of 4) would you give this answer? Look at the mark scheme in the Introduction (AO1). What are the reasons for the mark you have given?

5. Now swap your answer with your partner's and mark each other's responses. What mark (out of 4) would you give the response? Refer to the mark scheme and give reasons for the mark you award.

Sample student answer – the 5-mark question

1. Write and answer to the following question:

   Explain two reasons why Christians believe that helping those in need is part of their discipleship.

   You must refer to St Mark's Gospel in your answer.

   [5 marks]

2. Read the following student sample answer:

   "The first reason that I would give for Christians helping those in need is that they believe they will be following the example of Jesus. He spent his ministry helping those in need. A good example of this is the healing of the Syro-Phoenician woman's daughter. Jesus helped her as part of his mission, even though at first he did not seem to want to help her.

   Christians are supposed to spread the Gospel, like in the parable of the sower. They can do this by meeting the needs of others, physically and spiritually. A good modern example of this is Sylvia Wright, who sold everything she had to go to India to help those in need."

3. With a partner discuss the sample answer. Is the focus of the answer correct? Is anything missing from the answer? How do you think it could be improved?

4. What mark (out of 5) would you give this answer? Look at the mark scheme in the Introduction (AO1). What are the reasons for the mark you have given?

5. Now swap your answer with your partner's and mark each other's responses. What mark (out of 5) would you give the response? Refer to the mark scheme and give reasons for the mark you award.

Sample student answer – the 12-mark question

1. Write an answer to the following question:

    'The twelve disciples do not set a good example for believers today.'

    Evaluate this statement. In your answer you:
    *   should give reasoned arguments to support this statement
    *   should give reasoned arguments to support a different point of view
    *   should refer to St Mark's Gospel
    *   should refer to non-religious arguments
    *   should reach a justified conclusion.

    [12 marks]
    [+ 3 SPaG marks]

2. Read the following student sample answer:

    The disciples were not chosen from those you might expect. The first four were fishermen and they did not have training as religious teachers. Jesus chose them anyway. They set a good example for disciples though, because Mark says that they just left their nets and their families without hesitation and followed Jesus. I think lots of people today would at least have some questions or a problem with just going. They then stayed with Jesus throughout his ministry. In this they set a good example because they showed loyalty and commitment.

    However, some of the disciples did not set a good example. They did not understand always what Jesus was doing. For example, they tried to turn children away when they were being brought to Jesus. Judas betrayed Jesus in the Garden of Gethsemane. He was in league with the Jewish leaders and he took them to arrest Jesus – even kissing him as a sign of who Jesus was. This was not a good example.

    Peter too let Jesus down and did not set a good example. In the courtyard of the High Priest's house he denied that he knew Jesus when he was asked three times. Christians should show more commitment than that, even if he was frightened. Yet Peter was the one who recognised Jesus as the Messiah and this was very important.

    So in conclusion I would say that the disciples sometimes set a good example and other times they did not.

3. With a partner, discuss the sample answer. Consider the following questions:
    *   Does the answer focus on the questions asked?
    *   Does the answer refer to Mark's Gospel and if so what references are there?
    *   Is there an argument to support the statement and how well developed is it?
    *   Is there a different point of view offered and how well developed is that argument?
    *   Has the student written a clear conclusion after weighing up both sides of the argument?
    *   Are there logical steps in the argument?
    *   What is good about this answer?
    *   How do you think it could be improved?

4. What mark (out of 12) would you give this answer? Look at the mark scheme in the introduction (AO2). What are the reasons for the mark you have given?

5. Now swap your answer to the question with your partner's and mark each other's responses. What mark (out of 12) would you give their answer? Refer to the mark scheme and give reasons for the mark you award.

Practice questions

1 What was the name of the tax collector that Jesus called as a disciple?

A) Levi   **B)** Peter   **C)** James   **D)** John   **[1 mark]**

2 Give **two** ways in which Jesus demonstrated that he was committed to supporting those disregarded by society. **[2 marks]**

>  **Study tip**
>
> This question can be answered with just a phrase or a sentence. The 'ways' do not need development.

3 Explain **two** contrasting beliefs about the nature of the Kingdom of God in St Mark's Gospel. **[4 marks]**

>  **Study tip**
>
> In this answer you should aim to give examples from Mark's Gospel. This could be the question from the rich young man, the widow's offering at the Temple or the phrase 'camel through the eye of a needle'.

4 Explain **two** ways in which Jesus' acceptance of the children brought to him is important for Christians today. Refer to St Mark's Gospel in your answer. **[5 marks]**

>  **Study tip**
>
> You should aim to make distinct references to Mark's Gospel in your answer.

5 'The Kingdom of God cannot exist before death.'

Evaluate this statement. In your answer you:

- should give reasoned arguments to support this statement
- should give reasoned arguments to support a different point of view
- should refer to St Mark's Gospel
- may refer to non-religious arguments
- should reach a justified conclusion.   **[12 marks]**
     [+ 3 SPaG marks]

>  **Study tip**
>
> Read the statement carefully. There are a number of questions you may wish to consider in your answer. For example, can people experience being part of the Kingdom in life? What does the Parable of the Sower, for example, teach? Is the work of Christian aid agencies about bringing the Kingdom of God to people? If people approach faith like children, with innocence, will they experience the Kingdom of God? How do Christians in the twenty-first century understand the Kingdom of God? Make sure you include examples from Mark's Gospel.

Glossary

A

allegory: a story where the spiritual message is given using non-spiritual images, each of which can easily be replaced to show the true meaning

anoint: to put oil on the head to show that God has chosen a person

apostle: 'one who is sent out', the name given to those disciples who became leaders of the early Church

ascension: the event, 40 days after the resurrection, when Jesus returned to God, the Father, in heaven

B

baptism: an initiation ceremony using water

blasphemy: a religious offence that includes claiming to be God

C

call: the feeling that a person has to follow a particular lifestyle or career, very often linked to service (see also 'vocation' on page xx)

commission: the occasion after the resurrection of Jesus when he gave the disciples instructions about their future mission

covenant: The agreement between God and the Jews that he would be their God and they would be his people

crucifixion: 1. Roman method of execution by which criminals were fixed to a cross; 2. the execution and death of Jesus on Good Friday

D

disciple: 1. a follower of Jesus; 2. the term used for the followers of Jesus

discrimination: actions or behaviour that result from prejudice

E

exorcism: to drive out evil spirits

G

Gentile: someone who is not Jewish

gospel: literally 'good news'; refers to the good news of the teaching of Jesus but also to the four written books in the New Testament: Matthew, Mark, Luke and John

H

haemorrhage: bleeding which is persistent and potentially life threatening

Holy Communion: the giving of bread and wine as a memorial of Jesus in church services; also referred to as Eucharist (thanksgiving), Mass or The Lord's Supper

Holy Spirit: the third person of the Trinity whom Christians believe is the inspiring presence of God in the world

K

Kingdom of God: In the teaching of Jesus: 1. the reign of God on earth now 2. heaven, the afterlife

M

martyr: one who is a witness and often suffers or dies for their belief

Messiah (Christ): 'the anointed one'; a leader of the Jews who is expected to live on earth at some time in the future

Messianic Secret: a characteristic of Mark's Gospel where Jesus does not wish to be recognised as the Messiah

miracle: a seemingly impossible event, usually good, that cannot be explained by natural or scientific laws, and is thought to be the action of God

mystical experience: a religious event where people see and feel things that create a sense of awe and fascination

P

parable: a story with spiritual meaning told by Jesus to challenge listeners and teach them about their relationship with God

passion narrative: the part of Mark's Gospel which deals with the last week of Jesus' life

passion prediction: a passage in Mark's Gospel where Jesus explains that he will suffer and die

Passover: the Jewish festival held in the spring which commemorates the freeing of the Hebrew slaves from Egypt

prayer: communicating with God, either silently or through words of praise, thanksgiving or confession, or requests for God's help or guidance

prejudice: unfairly judging someone before the facts are known. Holding biased opinions about an individual or group

R

Rabbi: a Jewish teacher

ransom: usually a payment made to release a hostage. In Roman times, a payment made to get someone out of prison

repentance: saying sorry and a way of believers acknowledging to God that things have gone wrong

resurrection: 1. rising from the dead; 2. Jesus rising from the dead on Easter day. An event recorded in all four gospels and the central belief of Christianity

S

sabbath (shabbat): the Jewish holy day of the week; a day of spiritual renewal beginning at sunset on Friday and continuing to nightfall on Saturday

Sanhedrin: the Jewish Council at the time of Jesus. It consisted of 71 members, met in Jerusalem and was led by the High Priest

Satan: name for the Devil – the power and source of evil

Shema: a Jewish prayer affirming belief in the one God, found in the Torah

Son of God: a title used for Jesus, the second person of the Trinity; denotes the special relationship between Jesus and God the Father

Son of Man: a title that could refer to either just a human being, or a human who is given power by God

synagogue: a place of meeting for Jewish believers where the scrolls of the Law are kept

T

tax collectors: Jewish men who collected taxes on behalf of the Romans

transfiguration: the event in Mark's Gospel where Jesus is described as glowing dazzling white

transubstantiation: the belief that in the communion service the bread and wine change into the flesh and blood of Jesus

Twelve: the title given to Jesus' disciples as a group

U

universalism: the belief that God's Kingdom is for all, including those looked down on by others

V

vocation: to feel called by God to undertake an action, work or to follow a particular career

M

martyrs 42, 43
Maundy Thursday 31
medicine 79
Messiah ('anointed one') 10–11, 19, 23, 25,
    35, 41
Messianic Secret 10, 11, 19, 25, 60
miracles
    healing miracles 16–19, 32–3, 57,
        68–71, 78–9
    nature miracles 22–3, 57
mission 80–1
Montefiore, Hugh 77
Moses 26–7
Mount of Olives 35
Mustard Seed, Parable of 56–7
mystical experiences 26, 27

N

nature miracles 22–3, 57
neighbour, loving one's 63

O

Olives, Mount of 35
outcasts of society 64–75

P

Palestine 9, 66
Palm Sunday 35
parables of the
    Growing Seed 54–5
    Mustard Seed 56–7
    Sower 52–3
paralysed man, healing of 16–17
passion narrative 34–5
passion prediction 24, 25, 28–9

Passover 26, 36
Paul the Apostle 69
persecution of Christians 21, 83
Peter (disciple of Jesus) 9, 19, 25, 27,
    39, 83
    denials of 84–5
Pharisees 66, 67
Pilate, Pontius 42–3
possession by evil spirits 70–1
poverty 72
prayer 38–9, 57, 70, 71
prejudice 69

R

Rabbis 26, 58
ransoms 30
repentance 12
resurrection 46–7, 86
rich man, story of 60–1
Romans 9, 28, 39, 40, 42–3, 66

S

Sabbath (Shabbat) 20
Sadducees 82
Sanhedrin 40, 41
Satan 14, 25
Shema 62–3
Simon the leper 74, 75
sinners 66, 67
social outcasts 64–75
Son of God 10
Son of Man 10, 11, 17, 28, 41
Sower, Parable of the 52–3
suffering 25, 28, 31
symbolism
    anointing 74
    bread 23, 37

doves 14
fish 22, 23
water 13, 14
wine 37
synagogues 18, 19
Syro-Phoenician woman's daughter,
    healing of 68–9

T

tax collectors 66–7
Temple 72
temptations 14, 15, 25
Ten Commandments 61, 62–3
Thomas, Dr M.A. 65
transfiguration 26–7
transubstantiation 36, 37
treasury, widow at the 72–3
trial of Jesus 40–3
the Twelve 18, 19, 80–1

U

universalism 74, 75

V

vocations 30, 31
voice of God 15, 27

W

water symbolism 13, 14
wealth 60–1, 73
widow at the treasury 72–3
wine symbolism 37
woman with a haemorrhage 78–9
women 68–9, 72–5, 78–9

Z

Zealots 39, 54, 57